New Arrival English

Literacy and School Orientation

Jane A. Yedlin

Caroline T. Linse

New England Multifunctional Resource Center
for Language and Culture in Education
at Brown University

THOMSON
✳
™
HEINLE

Australia Canada Mexico Singapore Spain United Kingdom United States

Publisher: Stanley J. Galek
Editorial Director: Christopher Foley
Project Manager: Jennifer Bixby
Assistant Editors: Erik Gundersen, Margaret M. Morris
Editorial Production Manager: Elizabeth Holthaus
Production Editor: Kristin M. Thalheimer

Copy Editor: Kathy Sands Boehmer
Interior Art: Sean Sheerin, Gary Undercuffler
Photos: Stuart Cohen
Design and Composition: DECODE, Inc.
Manufacturing Coordinator: Jerry Christopher
Cover Design: Dorothea Sierra

Acknowledgements

The authors and publisher would like to acknowledge the contributions of the following individuals who reviewed or field tested *New Arrival English* at various stages of development and who offered many helpful insights and suggestions:

Carolyn Bernache
Prince George's County (MD)
Public Schools

Patricia Brys-Overeem
Culver City (CA) School District

Murkje deVries
Providence (RI) Public School
Department

Norma E. Hernandez
ESL Consultant

Michele Hewlett-Gomez
Sam Houston State University
Huntsville, TX

Karen Karten
Woonsocket (RI) High School

Angela Pantaleone
San Diego (CA) Unified School District
Newcomer Center

Michael Paul
Central Falls (RI) High School

Jeanne Perrin
Boston (MA) Public Schools

Leslie Rolph
San Diego (CA) High School

Kay Stark
Hartford (CT) Public Schools
New Arrival Center

Grace Valenzuela
Language and Multicultural Resources
Portland, ME

Catherine E. Walsh
New England Multifunctional
Resource Center
University of Massachusetts

We would also like to thank the people at Charlestown (MA) High School for their generosity, hospitality, and invaluable help. We would especially like to thank the following individuals: Stacey T. Johnson, Headmaster; Wendy Kwok Lee, Head, Bilingual Department; Peter K.C. Law, Bilingual Guidance Counselor; Gladys Agudelo; Jorgé A. Andina; and Azucena Yun Mei Li.

The authors wish to thank Heinle for their enthusiasm and for the painstaking attention to this project.

Dedicated to George, Max, and Jesse for their support and inspiration. JY
Thanks to Aunt Margaret for all of her assistance. CTL

Library of Congress Cataloging-in-Publication Data

Yedlin, Jane.
     New Arrival English: literacy and school orientation / Jane A. Yedlin,
Caroline T. Linse.
         p.   cm.
     ISBN 0-8384-2253-5
         1. English language—Textbooks for foreign speakers. 2. Language
and education—Problems, exercises, etc. 3. Schools—Problems, exercises, etc.
4. Readers—Schools. I. Linse, Caroline T. II. Title. III. Title: Literacy and
school orientation.
PE1128.Y45 1992   91–48143
428.2'4—dc20   CIP

ISBN 0-8384-2253-5

10 9 8 7 6

Contents

Preface   v

Literacy Foundations

Unit		Page	Signs (New Words)	New Letters	Math Concepts	Additional Receptive Aural/Oral Vocabulary
A	Signs at School	1	Bus, School, Stop	Bb, Cc, Hh, Ll, Oo, Pp, Ss, Tt, Uu		
B	In the Office	6	Office, Principal, Secretary, Telephone	Aa, Ee, Ff, Ii, Nn, Rr, Yy	Counting 1–5 • Number recognition • Writing numerals	Apple(s), bicycle(s), bus(es), car(s) circle(s), students(s)
C	Rooms in the School	13	Boys, Girls, Janitor, Teachers	Gg, Jj		
D	Inside the Restroom	18	No Smoking, Towels, Trash	Kk, Mm, Ww	Counting 1–10 • Number recognition • Writing numerals	Bag(s), banana(s), book(s) bus driver(s), notebook(s) orange(s), pen(s), pencil(s), triangle(s)
E	Helpful Places	25	Cafeteria, Library, Nurse, Quiet	Qq		
F	The Cafeteria	30	Hot Food, Ketchup, Milk, Sandwiches	Dd	Counting 1–20 • Number recognition • Writing numerals • Counting by 5's	Eraser(s), ruler(s), square(s), tee shirt(s)
G	The Gym	37	Gym, Locker Room, Showers			
H	Classrooms	42	Art, Computer Lab, Home Economics, Wood Shop		Counting 1–30 • Number recognition • Writing numerals • Counting by 5's, 10's	Doughnut(s), hamburger(s), hot dog(s), muffin(s) pear(s), pretzel(s)
I	Emergency	49	Exit, Fire Alarm, No Parking Zone, Van	Vv, Xx, Zz		
J	Around the School	54	Down, In, No, Out, Up, Yes		Counting 1–100 • Number Recognition • Writing Numerals • Counting by 5's, 10's	Chair(s)

Literacy in Action

Unit		Page	Language Goals	Literacy Goals	Math Lifeskills
1	Welcome to Central High School	63	Use greetings • Identify places, self, and others	Recognize and write familiar words in sentences	Recognize/write bus numbers
2	Give Information	67	Give personal information	Write name, address, phone number (on forms)	Recognize/write telephone and house numbers • Say *oh* for zero
3	Spell Your Name	73	Request clarification	Spell/write first and last name • Recognize letter names	
4	School Registration	79	Verify information	Write age and address • Use charts	Discriminate between *-tys* and *-teens*
5	Welcome to English Class	83	Take responsibility for classroom expectations, school rules, and supplies	Complete text by filling in blanks	Recognize use of room numbers to indicate floors (101=1st floor)
6	In the Classroom	88	Identify classroom objects as literacy tools • Identify friends	Complete crossword puzzle	
7	High School Classes	92	Identify school personnel and subjects • Give/ask for locations	Supply information on a schedule card • Use abbreviations: *Mr., Mrs., Ms., 1st, 2nd, 3rd*	Use room numbers to indicate floors (101=1st floor)
8	A School Day	98	Express location using *at, in,* and *on*	Use schedules as organizers for daily responsibilities	Tell time to the hour using digital and analog clocks
9	Follow Directions	102	Express non-comprehension • Ask for/give directions	Use *left* and *right* to express location and direction	Use odd/even numbers to locate rooms • Use numbers to open combination locks
10	School Schedules	106	Identify the days of the week and school expectations for punctuality • Apologize	Use time words appropriately	Tell time to the minute using digital and analog clocks
11	Friends at School	112	Identify places of origin, languages • Express likes and dislikes	Write about places of origin, languages, likes and dislikes • Use maps	
12	Write about Yourself	117	Identify months of the year, birthdays, and birthday customs	Review all personal and school information in writing	Express beginning and ending times of class periods
Word List		122			

Preface

To the Teacher

New Arrival English: Literacy and School Orientation is a complete instructional program for middle and high school students who have had no previous exposure to English. Many of these students have had their educations interrupted in their native countries. Others may be speakers of languages with oral traditions or with non-Roman alphabets. They require basic literacy and language skills, orientation to school, and modeling of appropriate student behaviors. The goal of the program is to provide a framework for acquiring these skills and behaviors and to help students find meaning and a sense of personal progress in their education.

Contents

New Arrival English develops language and literacy through a comprehension-based approach. Each unit opens with photographs presenting language in a school context. Students develop comprehension by listening to the instructor or the tape give a simple description of the photograph. However, students in multilevel classes should be encouraged to use their own words to talk about the photograph before they hear the description.

Following a natural progression, students respond non-verbally by pointing and circling before speaking. Students acquire a sight word vocabulary of the common school signs shown in the photographs, then progress to tracing and copying the signs. Students are gradually enabled to write about themselves.

New Arrival English has two distinct sections, Literacy Foundations and Literacy in Action.

Literacy Foundations helps students acquire or reinforce receptive skills. In this section, print is introduced through the words that students see on signs every day at school. In the context of whole words such as OFFICE, NURSE, QUIET, and CAFETERIA, all letters of the alphabet are presented and practiced in both upper and lower cases. In this section of *New Arrival English,* students receive both oral and written input as they join a new arrival student finding her way around the school. Each unit in Literacy Foundations is similar in format to provide the predictability and security that enables students to focus their attention on language and literacy skills.

Literacy in Action helps new arrival students use social and academic language to understand and function in the school environment. Students continue to acquire receptive skills and additional focus is placed on production. Activities provide students with the language necessary to interact effectively in school settings. The language and school survival skills practiced include: registration, greetings, following instructions, asking for feedback and clarification, asking for and offering help, initiating and participating in conversations, reading class schedules, identifying school subjects, taking responsibility for having essential school supplies, etc.

Basic math vocabulary and concepts are introduced in the Literacy Foundations section. Throughout the text students are exposed to math language in increasingly contextualized situations.

Using *New Arrival English* to Meet the Needs of Students at Different Levels

In recognition of the fact that there are multiple proficiency levels in any beginning ESL, pre-beginning, or literacy class, *New Arrival English* features three instructional options designed to meet the needs of students at differing stages of language acquisition and literacy development:

Option 1 is designed for preliterate students, students who lack literacy skills in their primary language or who speak a language with a non-Roman alphabet, and for students who speak very little or no English. Students at this level need to acquire literacy concepts and skills as well as develop beginning receptive language skills. They also require intensive direct instruction. The tape, and student book are used to introduce the material and model the exercises step by step. Students should be supervised closely and provided with immediate feedback.

Option 2 is designed for students who have some literacy skills in their primary language and for students who speak very little or no English. Students work on transferring their literacy skills from their primary language into English. Students are provided with a thorough review of the language and literacy skills presented in Literacy Foundations using the tape, and student book. Students receive direct instruction and interaction to work through the social and academic content covered in Literacy in Action by using the tape, picture cards, and student book. Follow up should be given with close supervision and feedback.

Option 3 is designed for students who speak some English and have some basic literacy skills in English. Students at this level need a solid background in language and literacy skills presented in Literacy Foundations and Literacy in Action. The content of each lesson is reinforced by using the tape, and student book. Students are able to work independently but should be monitored on a regular basis. Additional opportunities for students to expand upon the content covered in the book are highly recommended. In addition, students at this level may help their classmates by modelling language and literacy skills.

New Arrival English Instructional Options

	Literacy Foundations	Literacy in Action
	Receptive Oral/Aural School Based Language and Preliteracy Skills	Productive Oral/Aural School Based Language and Preliteracy Skills Personal Expression
Option 1 Preliteracy	Intensive Instruction	Continued Intensive Instruction
Option 2 Early Literacy	Guided Practice and Review	Intensive Instruction
Option 3 Beginning Literacy	Guided Practice and Review	Guided Practice and Review

The chart above illustrates the instructional options available for students at different levels.

Components of the *New Arrival English* Program

The components of *New Arrival English* are closely interconnected to provide students with a comprehensive introduction to oral and written English.

Student Book

The text focuses on the school environment, capitalizing on school routines to make language comprehensible. Motivation is increased by the immediate relevance of the book to the students' lives.

Tape Program

Descriptions, conversations, and listening exercises are all on the tapes that accompany *New Arrival English*. Scripts of the recorded material are included in the Instructor's Manual. In addition, cassette symbols in the student text mark the sections that are recorded.

Instructor's Manual and Assessment Program

The Instructor's Manual provides general guidelines for teaching oral and written English and school survival skills. Notes for each student-text page give practical suggestions for presenting and practicing new material. The manual also provides strategies for using the various program components to meet the needs of individual students at different levels. It also includes the Placement Test and Student Observation Checklist with instructions for administering the test and for recording student progress. The Placement Test helps select the appropriate instructional option for each student. The Student Observation Checklist helps organize an assessment portfolio to document each student's literacy development and second language acquisition.

Activity Masters

Illustrated Activity Masters, written for students at different levels, provide opportunities to reinforce and extend English language and literacy skills. The Activity Masters provide additional exercises for students at the very beginning level to practice the skills presented in the student book. They also challenge students at higher levels to reflect and write about their personal experiences.

Bibliography

Bell, J. and Burnaby, B., *A Handbook for ESL Literacy*. Toronto, Ontario: Ontario Institute for Students in Education, 1987.

Chang, Hedy Nai-Lin. *Newcomer Programs: Innovative Efforts to Meet the Educational Challenges of Immigrant Students*. San Francisco, California: California Tomorrow, 1990.

Freeman, Y. and Freeman, D. "Whole Language Approaches to Writing with Secondary Students of English as a Second Language," in Johnson and Roen (Eds.) *Richness in Writing: Empowering ESL Students*. White Plains, New York: Longman, 1989.

Goodman, K., and Y. and Hood, W. (Eds.) *The Whole Language Evaluation Book*. Portsmouth, New Hampshire: Heinemann Educational Books, Inc., 1989.

Smith, Frank, (Ed.) *Essays into Literacy*. Portsmouth: New Hampshire: Heinemann Educational Books, Inc. 1983.

Videotapes

Helping Refugees Learn to Read and Write, Washington D.C.: Center for Applied Linguistics, 1990.

PASS: Preparation for American Secondary Schools. Washington, D.C.: Center for Applied Linguistics, 1987.

Signs at School

A. Listen and point.

CENTRAL HIGH SCHOOL

SCHOOL BUS

STOP

Words

Bus

School

Stop

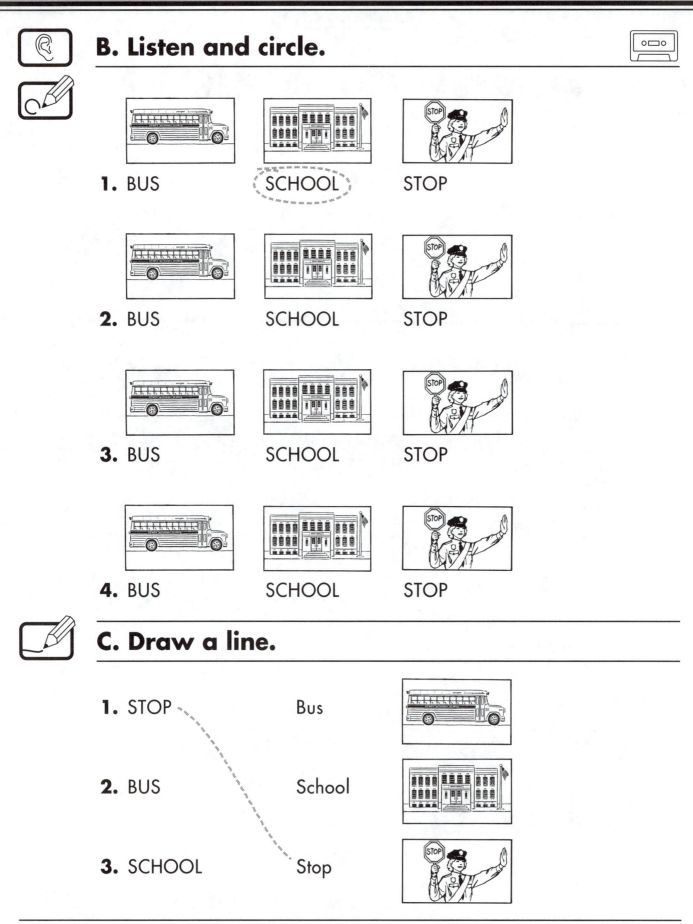

B. Listen and circle.

1. BUS (SCHOOL) STOP

2. BUS SCHOOL STOP

3. BUS SCHOOL STOP

4. BUS SCHOOL STOP

C. Draw a line.

1. STOP Bus

2. BUS School

3. SCHOOL Stop

2

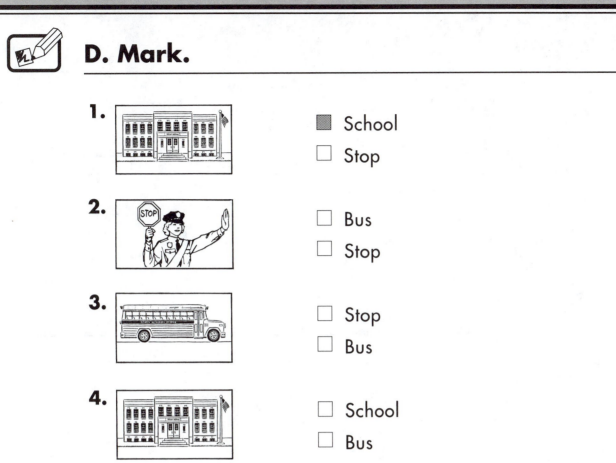

D. Mark.

1. ■ School
   ☐ Stop

2. ☐ Bus
   ☐ Stop

3. ☐ Stop
   ☐ Bus

4. ☐ School
   ☐ Bus

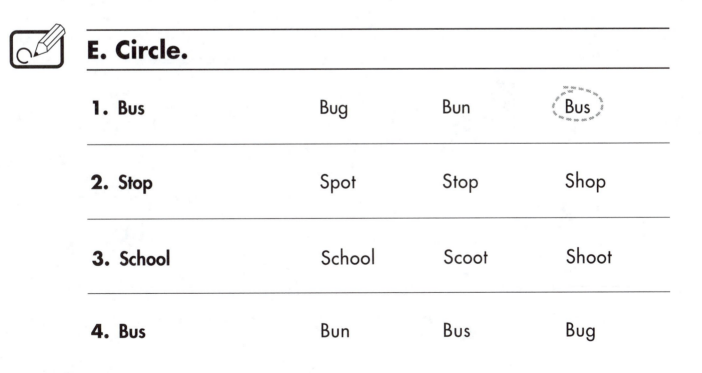

E. Circle.

1. Bus	Bug	Bun	Bus
2. Stop	Spot	Stop	Shop
3. School	School	Scoot	Shoot
4. Bus	Bun	Bus	Bug

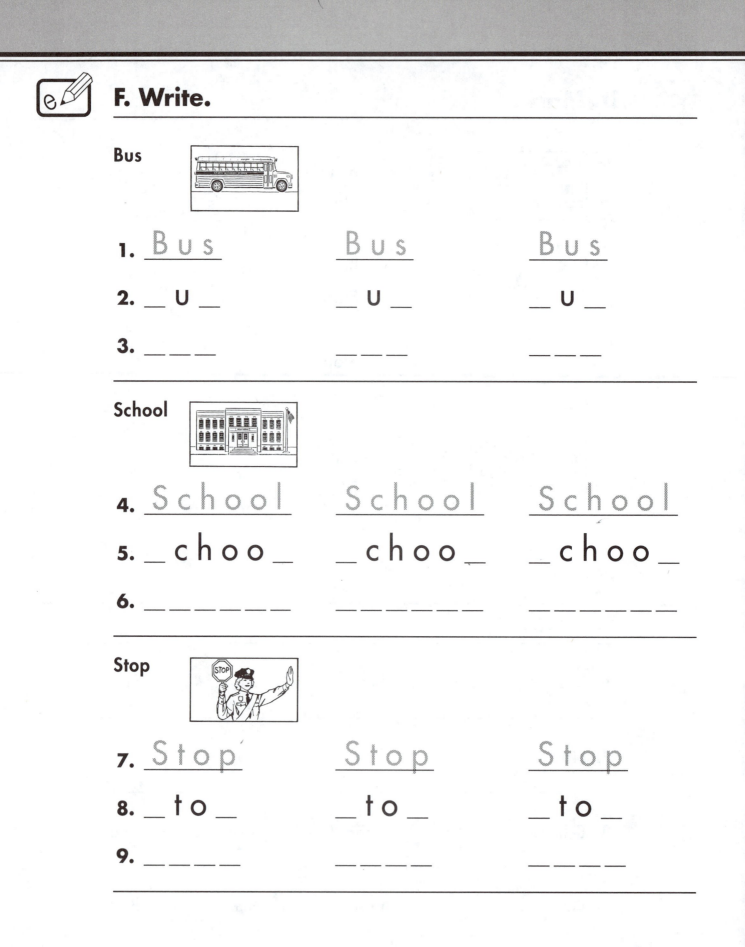

F. Write.

Bus

1. B u s   B u s   B u s

2. _ U _   _ U _   _ U _

3. _ _ _   _ _ _   _ _ _

School

4. S c h o o l   S c h o o l   S c h o o l

5. _ c h o o _   _ c h o o _   _ c h o o _

6. _ _ _ _ _ _   _ _ _ _ _ _   _ _ _ _ _ _

Stop

7. S t o p   S t o p   S t o p

8. _ t o _   _ t o _   _ t o _

9. _ _ _ _   _ _ _ _   _ _ _ _

G. Draw a line.

S   b

B   s

H. Write.

1. **S s**   S_   S_   S_   _s   _s   _s

2. **B b**   B_   B_   B_   _b   _b   _b

3. **S s**   S_   S_   S_   _s   _s   _s

4. **B b**   B_   B_   B_   _b   _b   _b

I. Write.

1. _____

2. _____

3. _____

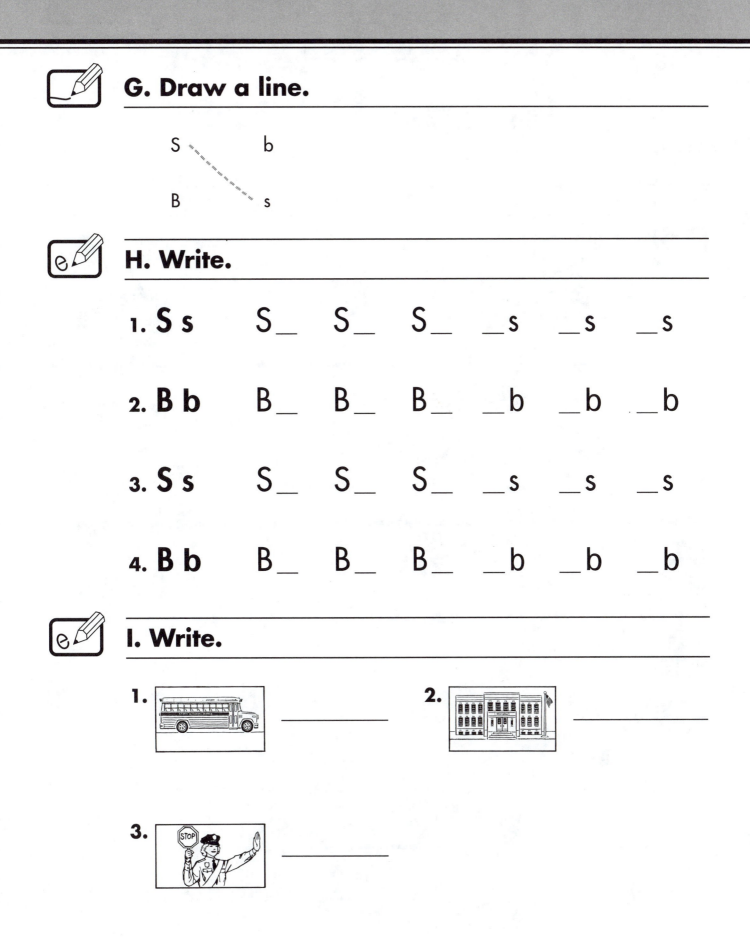

In the Office

A. Listen and point.

OFFICE
OF THE
PRINCIPAL

TELEPHONE

SECRETARY

Words

Office

Principal

Secretary

Telephone

B. Listen and circle.

1. SCHOOL   PRINCIPAL   SECRETARY   OFFICE

2. PRINCIPAL   BUS   OFFICE   TELEPHONE

3. OFFICE   STOP   SECRETARY   PRINCIPAL

4. TELEPHONE   PRINCIPAL   SECRETARY   OFFICE

C. Draw a line.

1. SECRETARY   Telephone

2. OFFICE   Secretary

3. TELEPHONE   Office

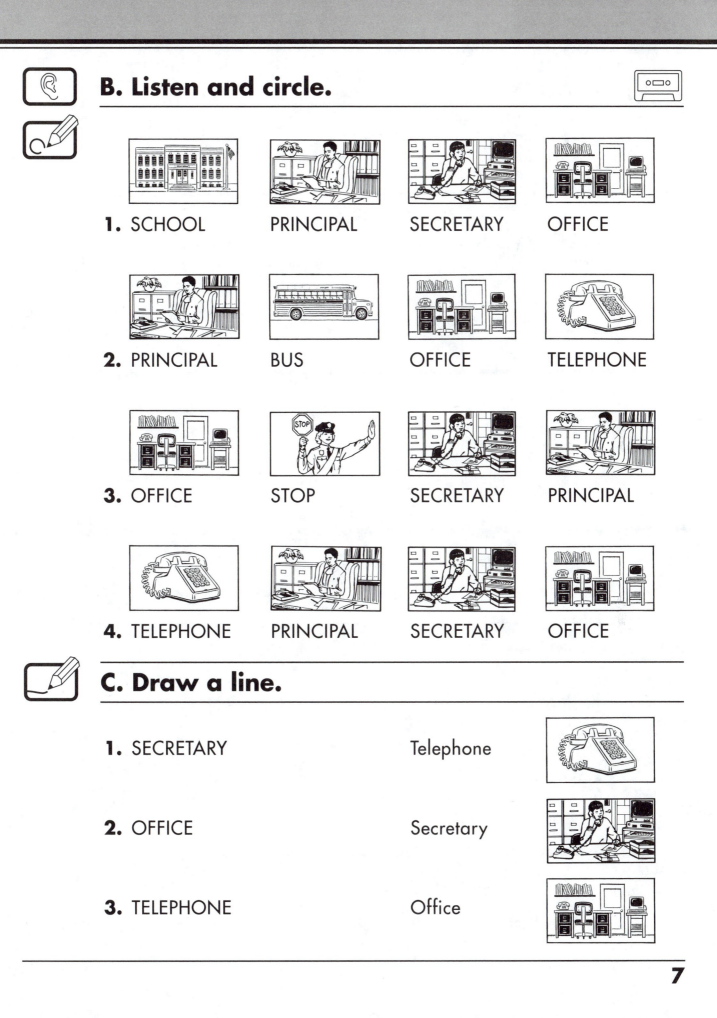

7

D. Mark.

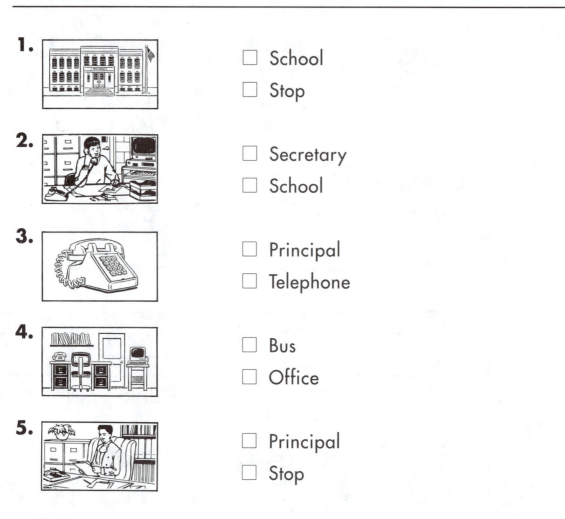

1. ☐ School
   ☐ Stop

2. ☐ Secretary
   ☐ School

3. ☐ Principal
   ☐ Telephone

4. ☐ Bus
   ☐ Office

5. ☐ Principal
   ☐ Stop

E. Circle.

1. **Principal**	Princess	Prince	Principal
2. **Office**	Officer	Office	Off
3. **Secretary**	Secret	Secretary	School
4. **Telephone**	Telephone	Telegraph	Television

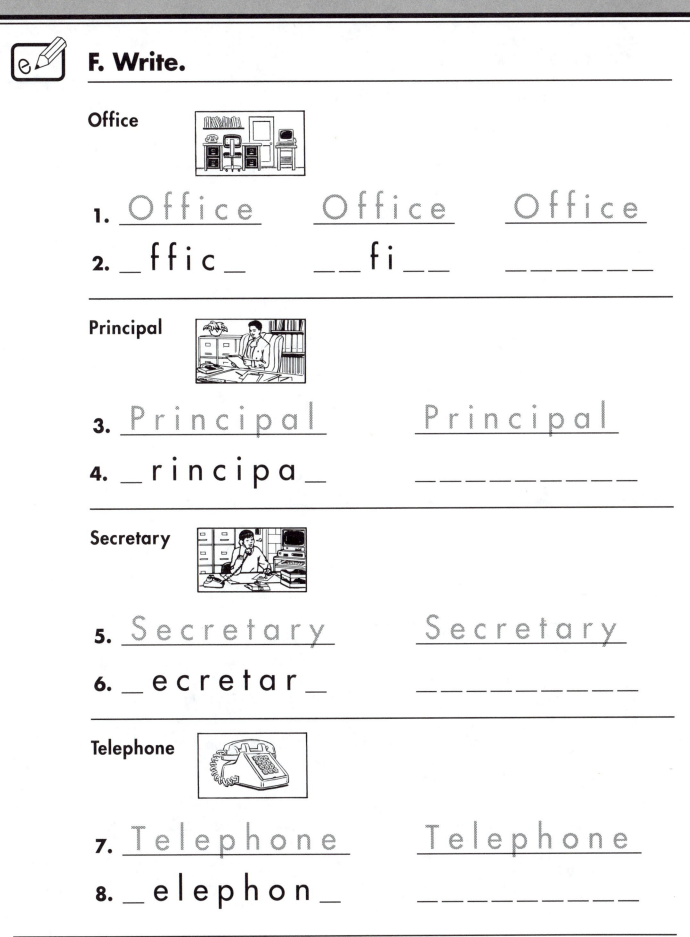

□✐ **F. Write.**

Office

1. <u>Office</u>   <u>Office</u>   <u>Office</u>

2. _ f f i c _   _ _ f i _ _   _ _ _ _ _ _

Principal

3. <u>Principal</u>   <u>Principal</u>

4. _ r i n c i p a _   _ _ _ _ _ _ _ _ _

Secretary

5. <u>Secretary</u>   <u>Secretary</u>

6. _ e c r e t a r _   _ _ _ _ _ _ _ _ _

Telephone

7. <u>Telephone</u>   <u>Telephone</u>

8. _ e l e p h o n _   _ _ _ _ _ _ _ _ _

G. Draw a line.

P   t

S   o

O   s

T   p

H. Write.

1. **P p** P_ P_ P_ _p _p _p

2. **O o** O_ O_ O_ _o _o _o

3. **T t** T_ T_ T_ _t _t _t

I. Write.

1. _____

2. _____

3. _____

4. _____

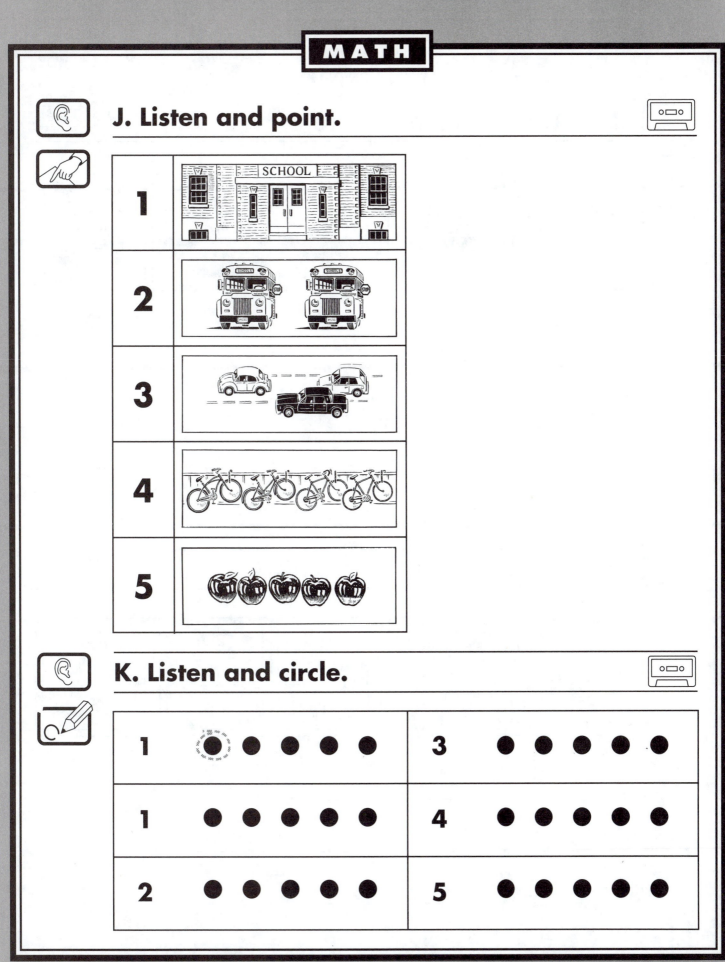

J. Listen and point.

1

2

3

4

5

K. Listen and circle.

1	● ● ● ● ●	3	● ● ● ● ●
1	● ● ● ● ●	4	● ● ● ● ●
2	● ● ● ● ●	5	● ● ● ● ●

L. Listen, point, and write.

| 1 | 2 | 3 | 4 | 5 |

M. Write.

Rooms in the School

A. Listen and point.

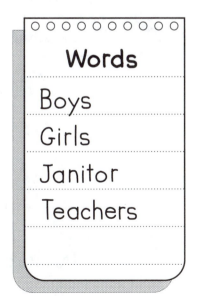

Words

Boys
Girls
Janitor
Teachers

B. Listen and circle.

1. PRINCIPAL   OFFICE   BOYS   SECRETARY

2. BOYS   JANITOR   TEACHERS   GIRLS

3. TEACHERS   GIRLS   JANITOR   BOYS

4. JANITOR   BOYS   GIRLS   TEACHERS

C. Draw a line.

1. GIRLS   Janitor

2. BOYS   Girls

3. JANITOR   Boys

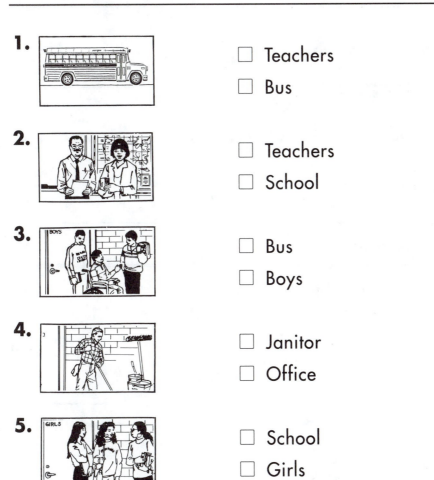

D. Mark.

1.
☐ Teachers
☐ Bus

2.
☐ Teachers
☐ School

3.
☐ Bus
☐ Boys

4.
☐ Janitor
☐ Office

5.
☐ School
☐ Girls

E. Circle.

1. Boys	Bugs	Boys	Bags
2. Girls	Girls	Girl	Grill
3. Janitor	Juniors	Junior	Janitor
4. Teachers	Teaching	Teachers	Teach

F. Write.

Girls

1. Girls   Girls   Girls

2. _ i r l _   _ i r l _   _ _ _ _ _

Boys

3. Boys   Boys   Boys

4. _ o y _   _ o y _   _ _ _ _

Teachers

5. Teachers   Teachers

6. _ e a c h e r _   _ _ _ _ _ _ _ _

Janitor

7. Janitor   Janitor

8. _ _ n i t o _   _ _ _ _ _ _ _

B   j

G   t

T   b

J   g

H. Write.

1. **G g**   G_   G_   G_   _g   _g   _g

2. **T t**   T_   T_   T_   _t   _t   _t

3. **J j**   J_   J_   J_   _j   _j   _j

4. **B b**   B_   B_   B_   _b   _b   _b

I. Write.

1. _____

2. _____

3. _____

4. _____

Inside the Restroom

A. Listen and point.

Words

No Smoking

Towels

Trash

B. Listen and circle.

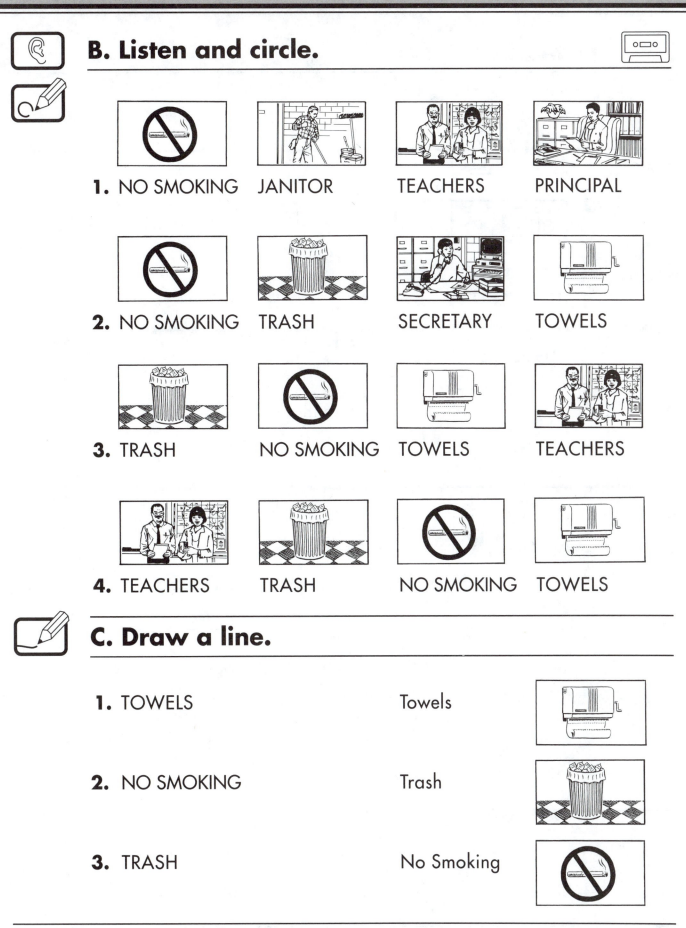

1. NO SMOKING   JANITOR   TEACHERS   PRINCIPAL

2. NO SMOKING   TRASH   SECRETARY   TOWELS

3. TRASH   NO SMOKING   TOWELS   TEACHERS

4. TEACHERS   TRASH   NO SMOKING   TOWELS

C. Draw a line.

1. TOWELS   Towels

2. NO SMOKING   Trash

3. TRASH   No Smoking

D. Mark.

1.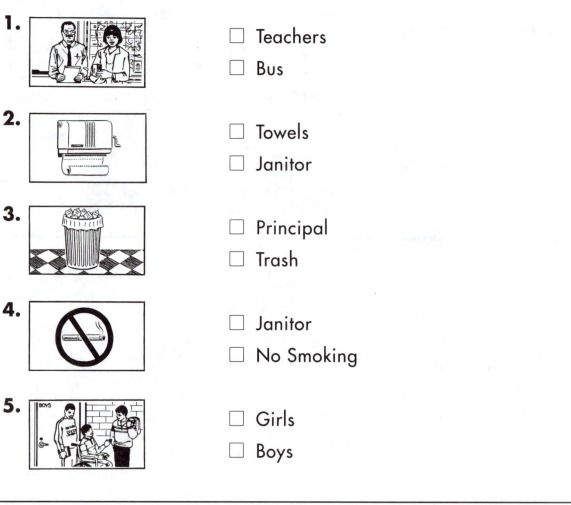
☐ Teachers
☐ Bus

2.
☐ Towels
☐ Janitor

3.
☐ Principal
☐ Trash

4.
☐ Janitor
☐ No Smoking

5.
☐ Girls
☐ Boys

E. Circle.

1. Boys	Bugs	Bags	Boys
2. Trash	Crash	Truck	Trash
3. No Smoking	No Smoking	No Eating	No Parking
4. Towels	Towers	Towels	Towns

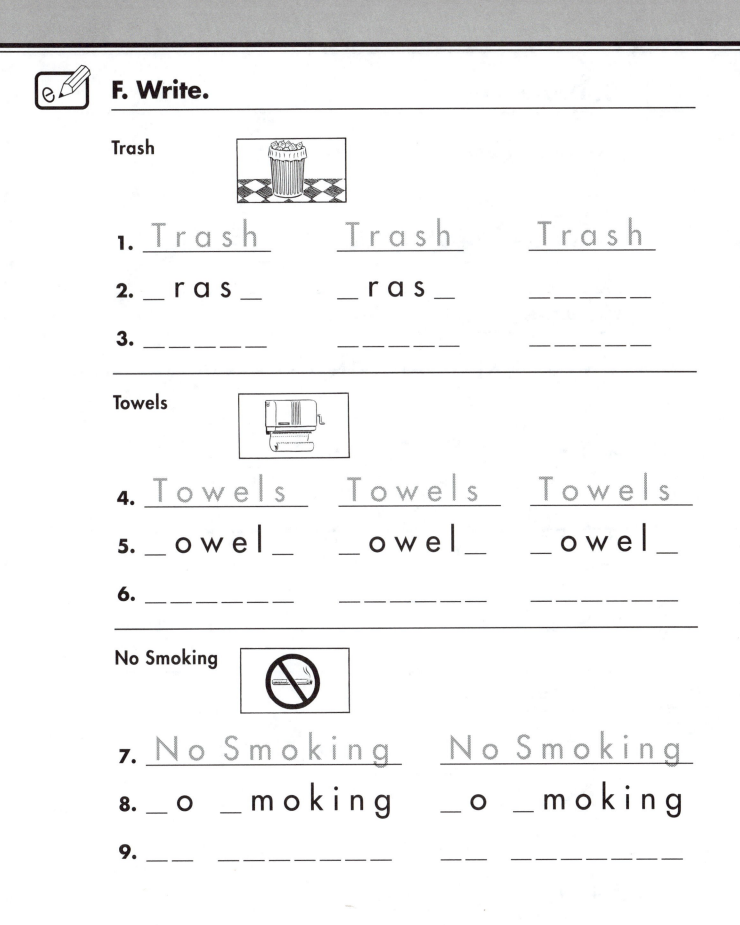

F. Write.

Trash

1. Trash   Trash   Trash

2. _ r a s _   _ r a s _   _ _ _ _ _

3. _ _ _ _ _   _ _ _ _ _   _ _ _ _ _

Towels

4. Towels   Towels   Towels

5. _ o w e l _   _ o w e l _   _ o w e l _

6. _ _ _ _ _ _   _ _ _ _ _ _   _ _ _ _ _ _

No Smoking

7. No Smoking   No Smoking

8. _ o _ m o k i n g   _ o _ m o k i n g

9. _ _ _ _ _ _ _ _   _ _ _ _ _ _ _ _

G. Draw a line.

S   t

N   s

T   n

H. Write.

1. **N n**   N_   N_   N_   _n   _n   _n

2. **T t**   T_   T_   T_   _t   _t   _t

3. **S s**   S_   S_   S_   _s   _s   _s

4. **G g**   G_   G_   G_   _g   _g   _g

I. Write.

1. _____

2. _____

3. _____

J. Listen and point.

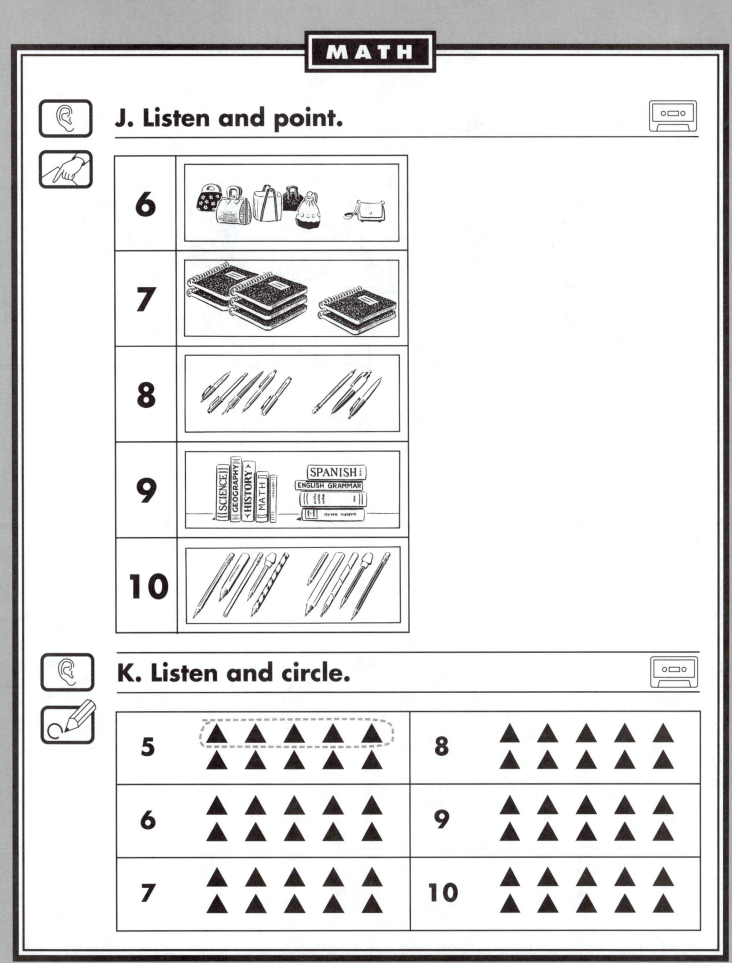

6

7

8

9

10

K. Listen and circle.

5

8

6

9

7

10

L. Listen, point, and write.

| 6 | 7 | 8 | 9 | 10 |

M. Write.

10

Helpful Places

A. Listen and point.

QUIET, PLEASE!

LIBRARY
HOURS
8:00 a.m. -
3:00 p.m.

NURSE

CAFETERIA

Words

Cafeteria

Library

Nurse

Quiet

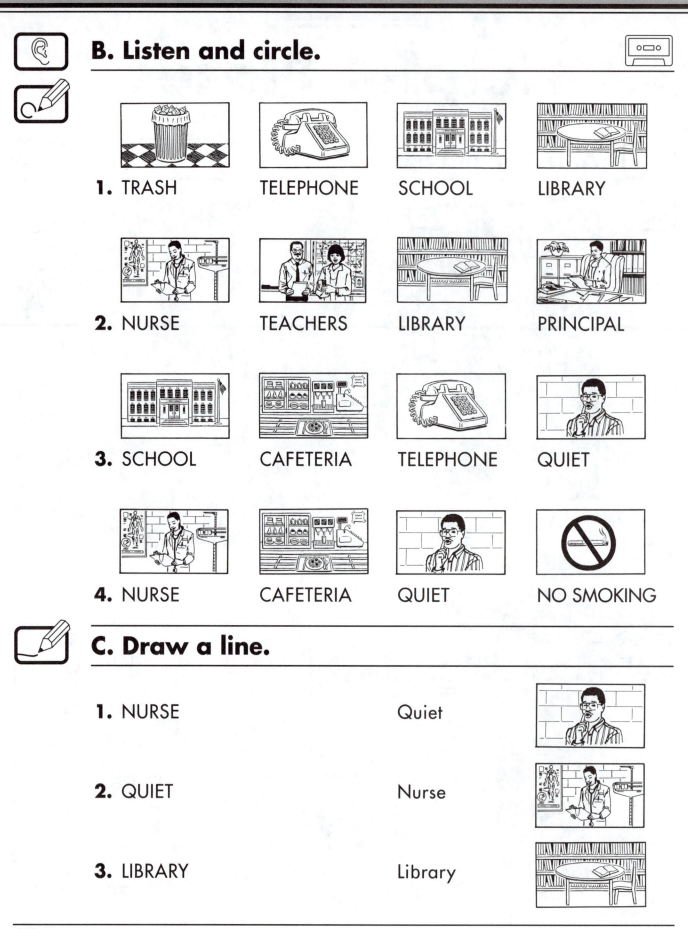

1. TRASH   TELEPHONE   SCHOOL   LIBRARY

2. NURSE   TEACHERS   LIBRARY   PRINCIPAL

3. SCHOOL   CAFETERIA   TELEPHONE   QUIET

4. NURSE   CAFETERIA   QUIET   NO SMOKING

C. Draw a line.

1. NURSE   Quiet

2. QUIET   Nurse

3. LIBRARY   Library

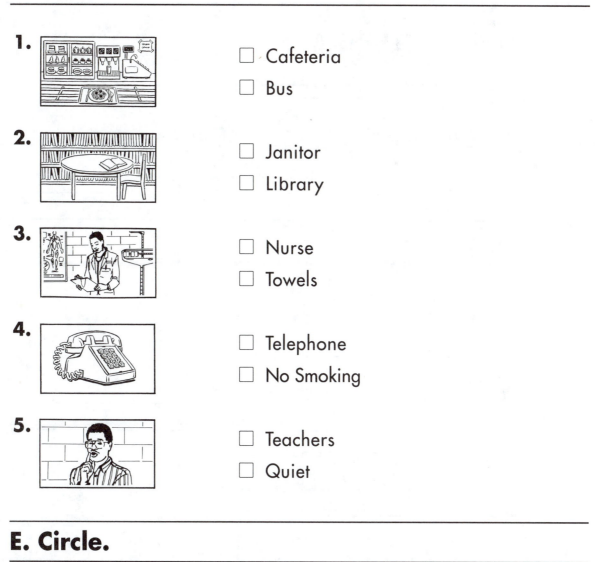

D. Mark.

1.
☐ Cafeteria
☐ Bus

2.
☐ Janitor
☐ Library

3.
☐ Nurse
☐ Towels

4.
☐ Telephone
☐ No Smoking

5.
☐ Teachers
☐ Quiet

E. Circle.

1. Nurse	Nose	Noise	Nurse
2. Cafeteria	Cafe	Cafeteria	Closet
3. Library	Librarian	Library	Libraries
4. Quiet	Quilt	Quite	Quiet

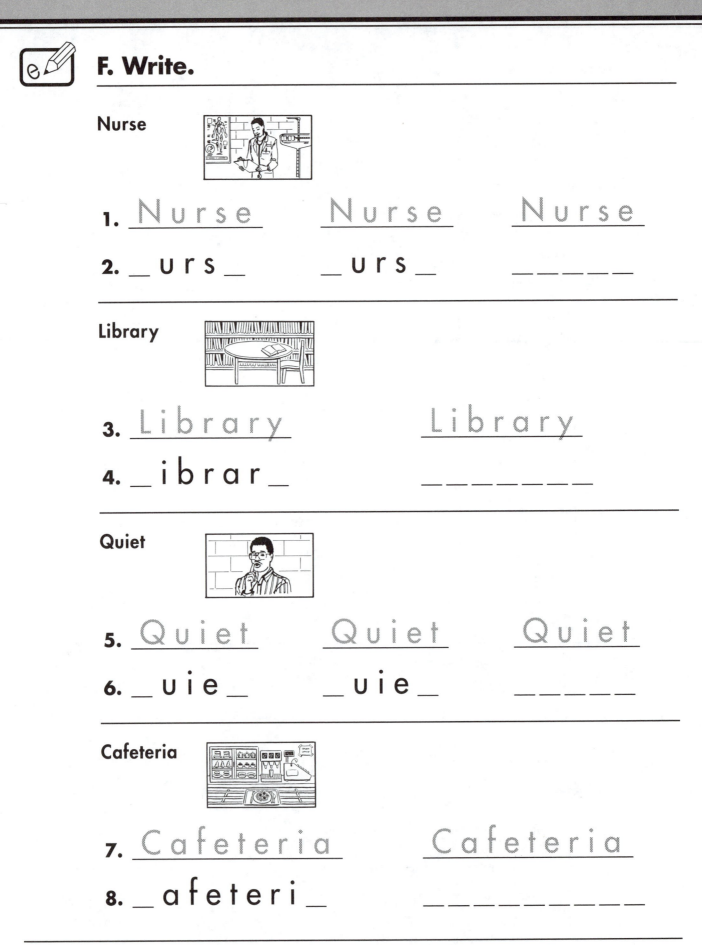

F. Write.

Nurse

1. Nurse   Nurse   Nurse

2. _ u r s _   _ u r s _   _ _ _ _ _ _

Library

3. Library   Library

4. _ i b r a r _   _ _ _ _ _ _ _

Quiet

5. Quiet   Quiet   Quiet

6. _ u i e _   _ u i e _   _ _ _ _ _

Cafeteria

7. Cafeteria   Cafeteria

8. _ a f e t e r i _   _ _ _ _ _ _ _ _

G. Draw a line.

N   q

L   c

C   l

Q   n

H. Write.

1. C c   C_   _c   C_   _c   C_   _c

2. L l   L_   _l   L_   _l   L_   _l

3. Q q   Q_   _q   Q_   _q   Q_   _q

4. N n   N_   _n   N_   _n   N_   _n

I. Write.

1. _____

2. _____

3. _____

4. _____

The Cafeteria

A. Listen and point.

MILK

SANDWICHES

HOT FOOD

KETCHUP

Words

Hot Food

Ketchup

Milk

Sandwiches

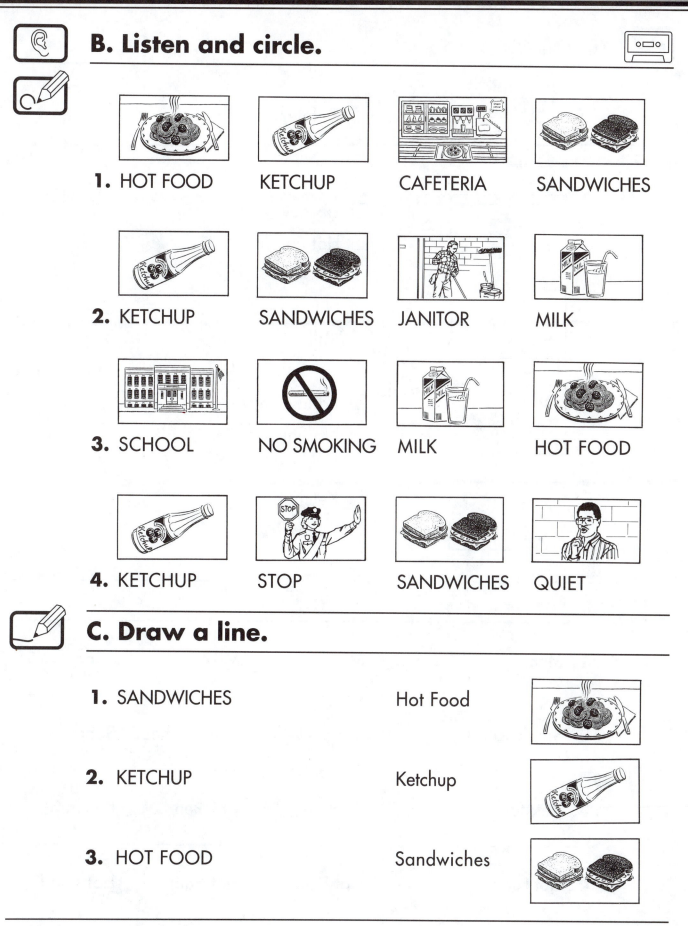

B. Listen and circle.

1. HOT FOOD   KETCHUP   CAFETERIA   SANDWICHES

2. KETCHUP   SANDWICHES   JANITOR   MILK

3. SCHOOL   NO SMOKING   MILK   HOT FOOD

4. KETCHUP   STOP   SANDWICHES   QUIET

C. Draw a line.

1. SANDWICHES   Hot Food

2. KETCHUP   Ketchup

3. HOT FOOD   Sandwiches

D. Mark.

1.
- ☐ Cafeteria
- ☐ Bus

2.
- ☐ Library
- ☐ Hot Food

3.
- ☐ Nurse
- ☐ Milk

4.
- ☐ Sandwiches
- ☐ No Smoking

5.
- ☐ Ketchup
- ☐ Quiet

E. Circle.

1. Milk	Milk	Mike	Mine
2. Sandwiches	Sand	Sandwiches	Sandwich
3. Ketchup	Kitchen	Chicken	Ketchup
4. Hot Food	Hot Dog	Hot Shot	Hot Food

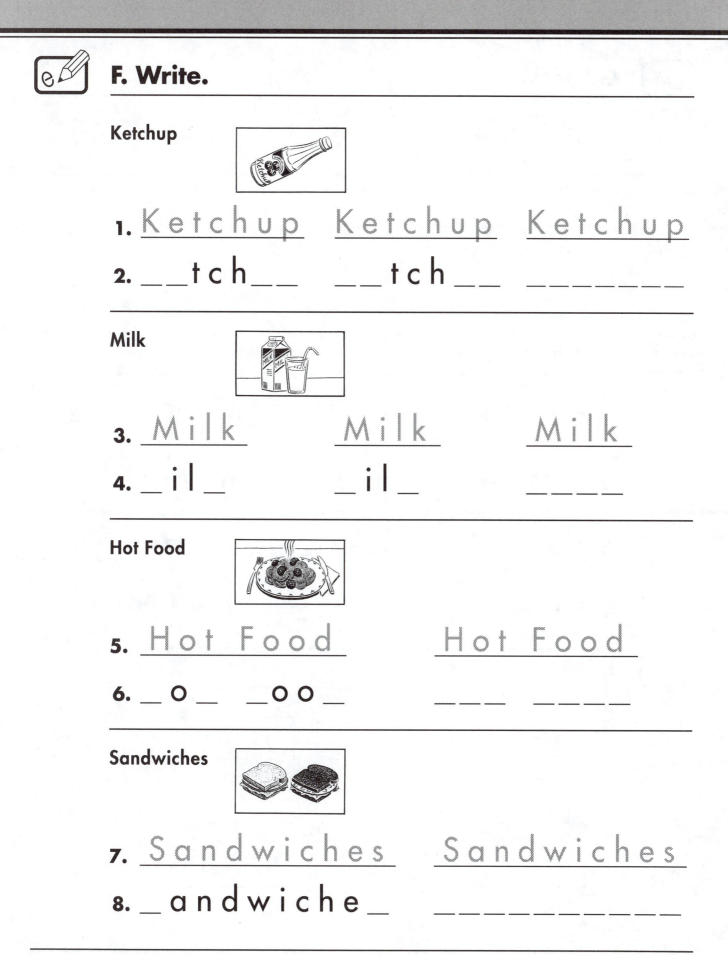

F. Write.

Ketchup

1. Ketchup Ketchup Ketchup

2. __ t c h __ __ t c h __ _____

Milk

3. Milk Milk Milk

4. _ i l _ _ i l _ ____

Hot Food

5. Hot Food Hot Food

6. _ o _ _ o o _ ___ ____

Sandwiches

7. Sandwiches Sandwiches

8. _ a n d w i c h e _ _____

G. Draw a line.

K   f

M   k

H   h

F   m

H. Write.

1. **K k**   K_   _k   K_   _k   K_   _k

2. **M m**   M_   _m   M_   _m   M_   _m

3. **H h**   H_   _h   H_   _h   H_   _h

4. **F f**   F_   _f   F_   _f   F_   _f

I. Write.

1. _____

2. _____

3. _____

4. _____

J. Listen, point, and write.

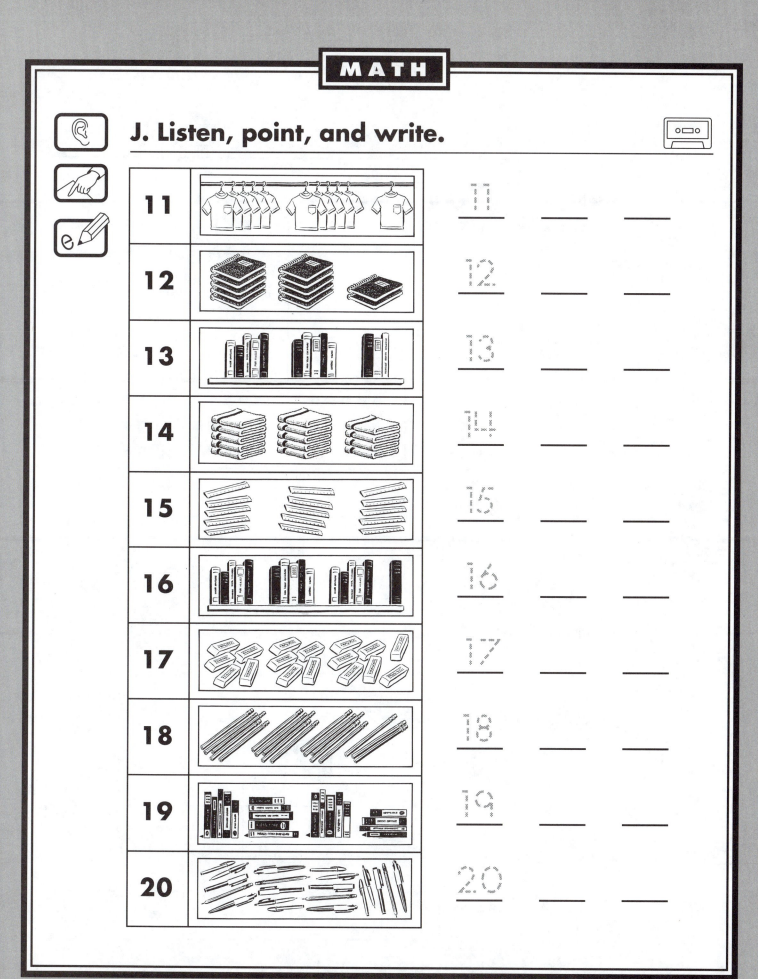

11		11		
12		12		
13		13		
14		14		
15		15		
16		16		
17		17		
18		18		
19		19		
20		20		

K. Write.

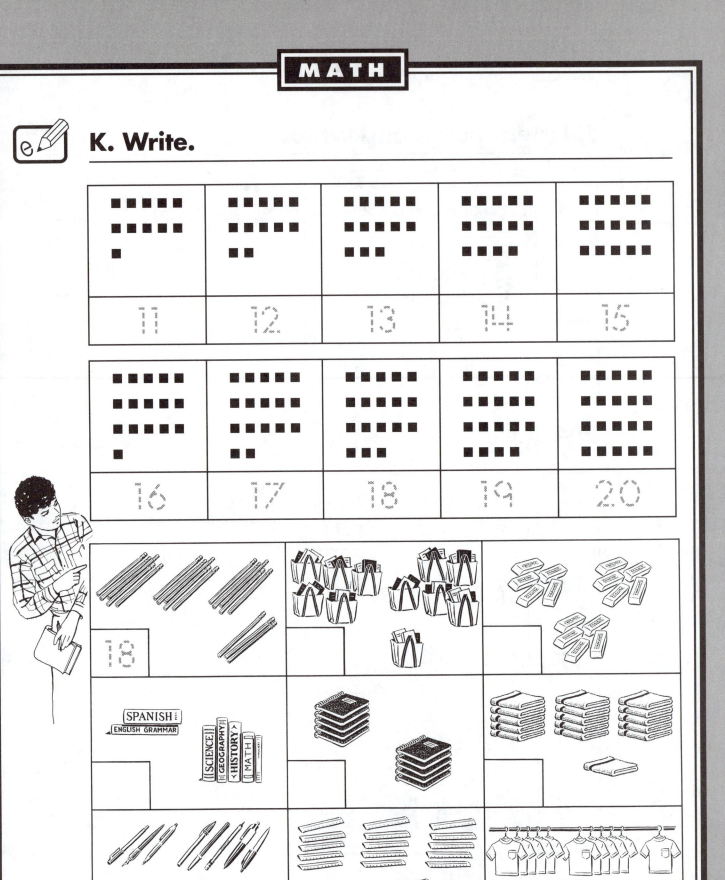

11	12	13	14	15

16	17	18	19	20

18

SPANISH
ENGLISH GRAMMAR
SCIENCE GEOGRAPHY HISTORY MATH

The Gym

A. Listen and point.

Words

Gym

Locker Room

Showers

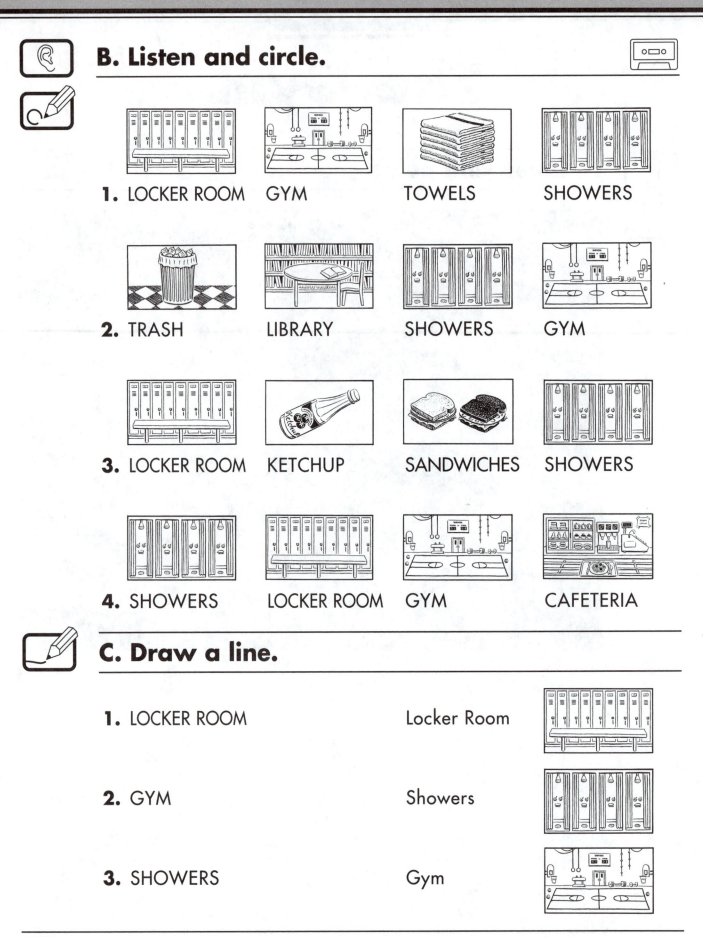

B. Listen and circle.

1. LOCKER ROOM   GYM   TOWELS   SHOWERS

2. TRASH   LIBRARY   SHOWERS   GYM

3. LOCKER ROOM   KETCHUP   SANDWICHES   SHOWERS

4. SHOWERS   LOCKER ROOM   GYM   CAFETERIA

C. Draw a line.

1. LOCKER ROOM   Locker Room

2. GYM   Showers

3. SHOWERS   Gym

D. Mark.

1.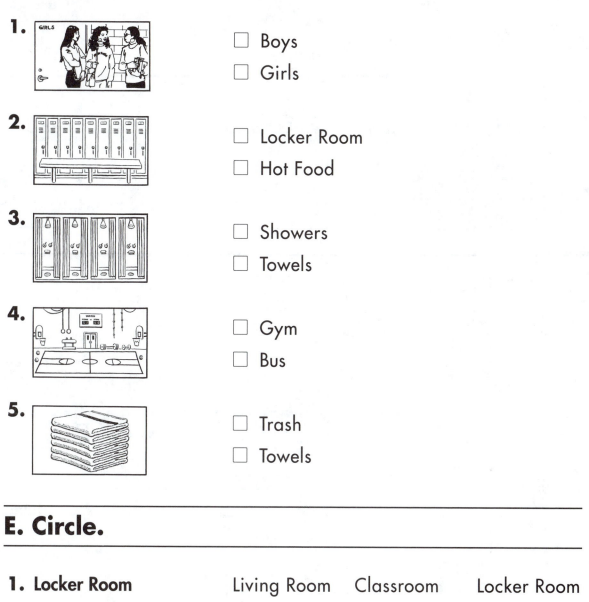
☐ Boys
☐ Girls

2.
☐ Locker Room
☐ Hot Food

3.
☐ Showers
☐ Towels

4.
☐ Gym
☐ Bus

5.
☐ Trash
☐ Towels

E. Circle.

1. Locker Room	Living Room	Classroom	Locker Room
2. Gym	Gum	Gym	Game
3. Showers	Slower	Showers	Shower

F. Write.

Gym

1. <u>Gym</u>   <u>Gym</u>   <u>Gym</u>   <u>Gym</u>

2. _ y _   _ y _   _ y _   _ y _

3. _ _ _   _ _ _   _ _ _   _ _ _

Locker Room

4. <u>Locker Room</u>   <u>Locker Room</u>

5. _ ocke_ _ oo_   _ ocke_ _ oo_

6. _ _ _ _ _ _ _ _ _ _ _   _ _ _ _ _ _ _ _ _ _ _

Showers

7. <u>Showers</u>   <u>Showers</u>

8. _ howe_ _   _ howe_ _

9. _ _ _ _ _ _ _   _ _ _ _ _ _ _

G. Draw a line.

L   s

R   r

G   l

S   g

H. Write.

1. **L l**   L_   _l   L_   _l   L_   _l

2. **R r**   R_   _r   R_   _r   R_   _r

3. **S s**   S_   _s   S_   _s   S_   _s

4. **G g**   G_   _g   G_   _g   G_   _g

I. Write.

1.   _____

2.   _____

3.   _____

UNIT H

Classrooms

 A. Listen and point.

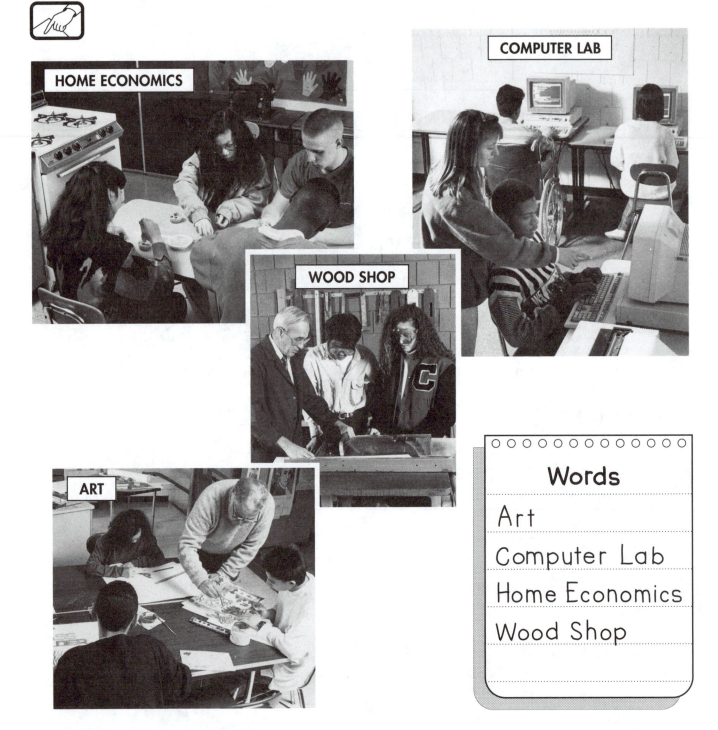

HOME ECONOMICS

COMPUTER LAB

WOOD SHOP

ART

Words
Art
Computer Lab
Home Economics
Wood Shop

B. Listen and circle.

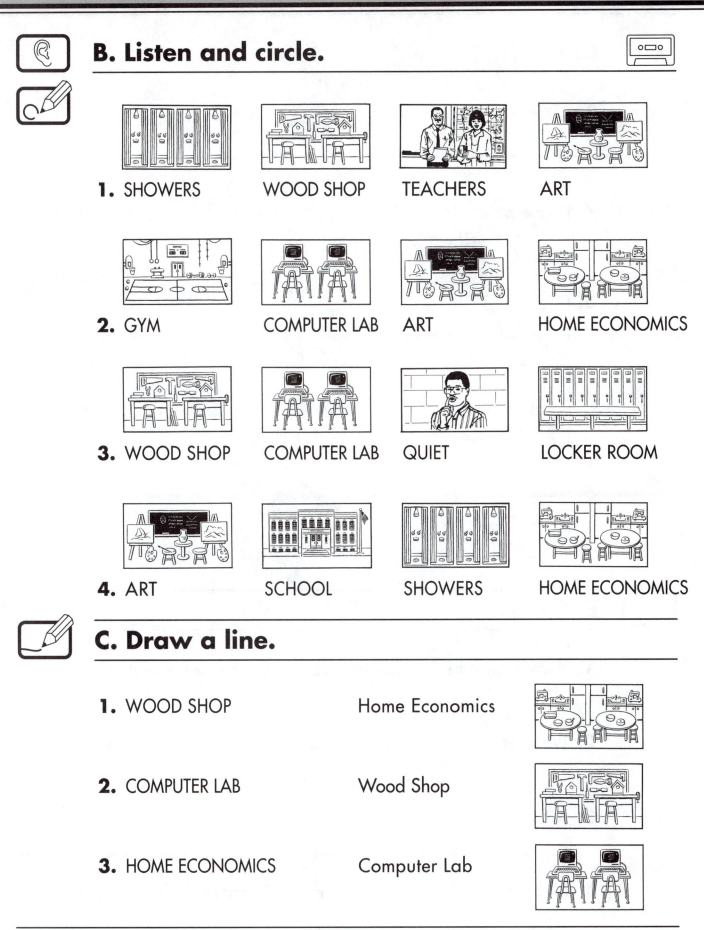

1. SHOWERS   WOOD SHOP   TEACHERS   ART

2. GYM   COMPUTER LAB   ART   HOME ECONOMICS

3. WOOD SHOP   COMPUTER LAB   QUIET   LOCKER ROOM

4. ART   SCHOOL   SHOWERS   HOME ECONOMICS

C. Draw a line.

1. WOOD SHOP   Home Economics

2. COMPUTER LAB   Wood Shop

3. HOME ECONOMICS   Computer Lab

D. Mark.

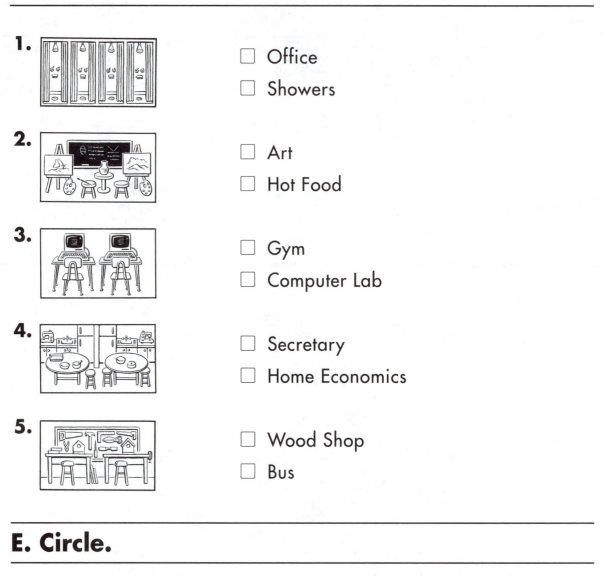

1.
- ☐ Office
- ☐ Showers

2.
- ☐ Art
- ☐ Hot Food

3.
- ☐ Gym
- ☐ Computer Lab

4.
- ☐ Secretary
- ☐ Home Economics

5.
- ☐ Wood Shop
- ☐ Bus

E. Circle.

1. Home Economics	Economics	Home Economics	Home
2. Wood Shop	Wood Shed	Card Shop	Wood Shop
3. Art	Card	Art	Artist
4. Computer Lab	Commuter	Computer Lab	Laboratory

F. Write.

Home Economics

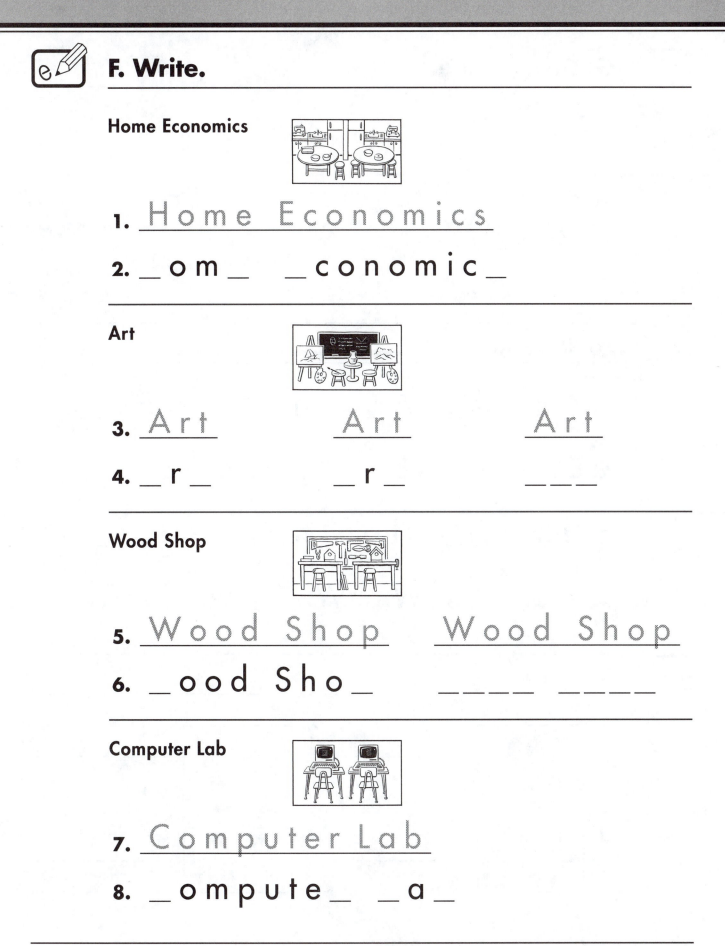

1. Home Economics

2. _ o m _   _ c o n o m i c _

Art

3. Art   Art   Art

4. _ r _   _ r _   _ _ _

Wood Shop

5. Wood Shop   Wood Shop

6. _ o o d   S h o _   _ _ _ _   _ _ _ _

Computer Lab

7. Computer Lab

8. _ o m p u t e _   _ a _

W   h

E   w

A   e

H   a

✏️ **H. Write.**

1. **A a**   A_   A_   _a   A_   _a   _a

2. **E e**   _e   E_   _e   _e   E_   E_

3. **H h**   H_   H_   _h   _h   H_   _h

4. **W w**   _w   W_   W_   _w   _w   W_

✏️ **I. Write.**

1.

2.

3.

4.

J. Listen, point, and write.

21		21 __ __
22		22 __ __
23		23 __ __
24		24 __ __
25		25 __ __
26		26 __ __
27		27 __ __
28		28 __ __
29		29 __ __
30		30 __ __

K. Write.

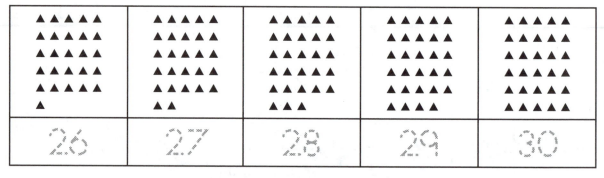

21　22　23　24　25

26　27　28　29　30

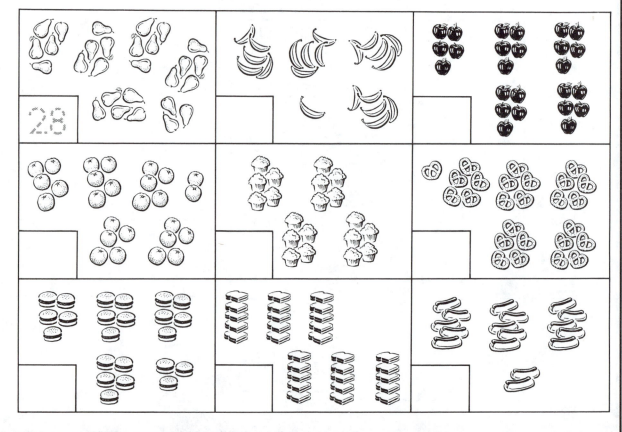

23

Emergency

A. Listen and point.

Words
Exit
Fire Alarm
No Parking Zone
Van

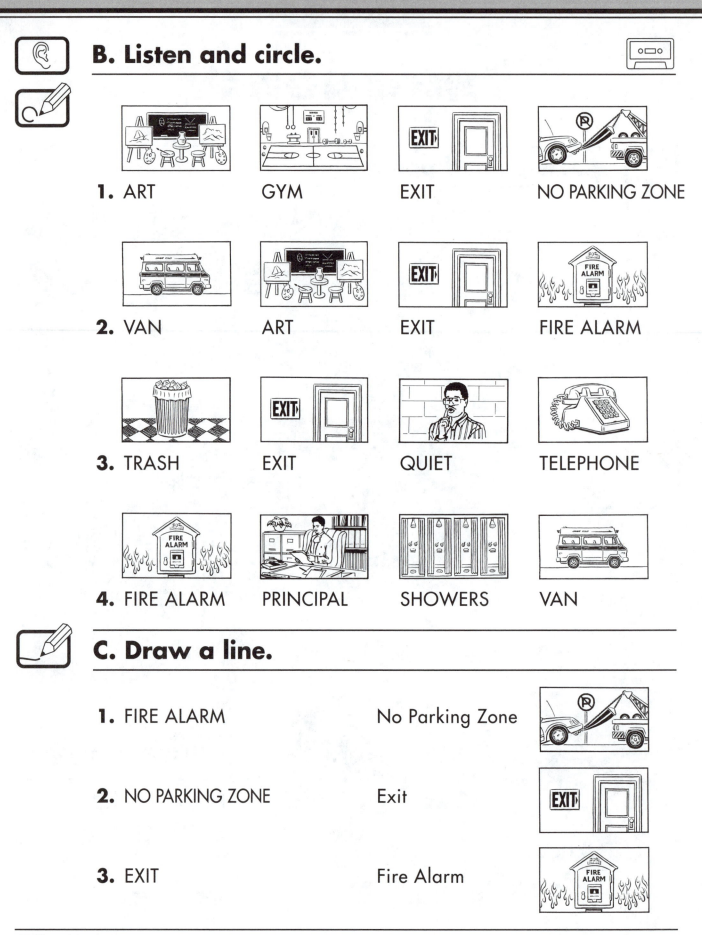

B. Listen and circle.

1. ART   GYM   EXIT   NO PARKING ZONE

2. VAN   ART   EXIT   FIRE ALARM

3. TRASH   EXIT   QUIET   TELEPHONE

4. FIRE ALARM   PRINCIPAL   SHOWERS   VAN

C. Draw a line.

1. FIRE ALARM   No Parking Zone

2. NO PARKING ZONE   Exit

3. EXIT   Fire Alarm

D. Mark.

1. ☐ Wood Shop
   ☐ Computer Lab

2. ☐ No Parking Zone
   ☐ Hot Food

3. ☐ Office
   ☐ Exit

4. ☐ Fire Alarm
   ☐ Home Economics

5. ☐ Van
   ☐ Bus

E. Circle.

1. Fire Alarm	First Alarm	Fast Alarm	Fire Alarm
2. Van	Can	Hand	Van
3. No Parking	No Parking	No Smoking	No Eating
4. Exit	Extra	Exit	Excellent

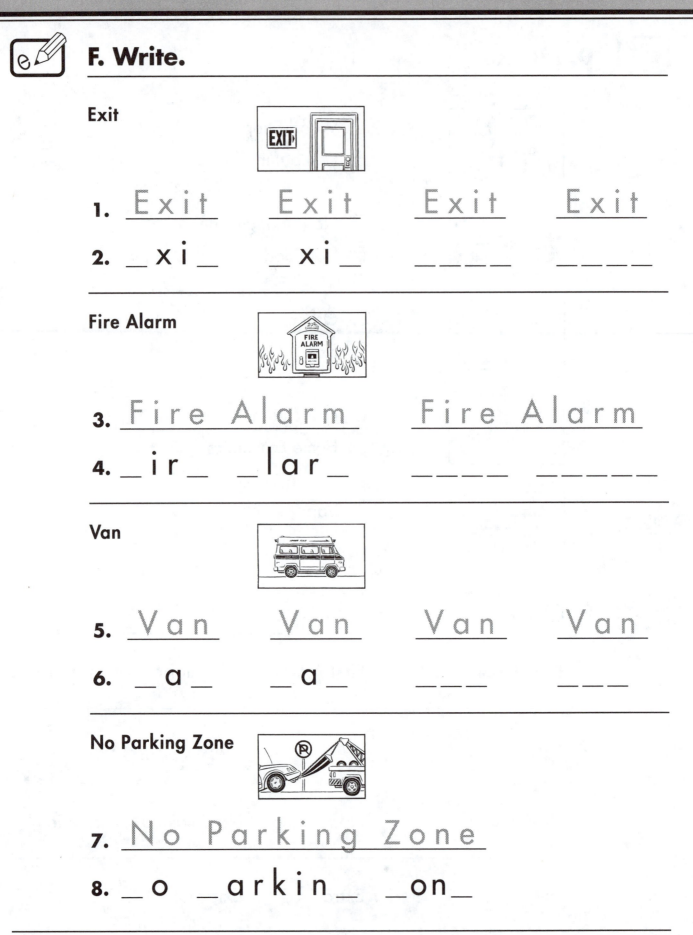

F. Write.

Exit

1. Exit   Exit   Exit   Exit

2. _ x i _   _ x i _   ____   ____

Fire Alarm

3. Fire Alarm   Fire Alarm

4. _ i r _ _ l a r _   ____ _____

Van

5. Van   Van   Van   Van

6. _ a _   _ a _   ___   ___

No Parking Zone

7. No Parking Zone

8. _ o _ a r k i n _ _ o n _

G. Draw a line.

E   v

V   x

Z   e

X   z

H. Write.

1. **X x**   X_   _x   _x   _x   X_   X_

2. **E e**   E_   E_   _e   E_   _e   _e

3. **Z z**   _z   _z   Z_   _z   Z_   Z_

4. **V v**   _v   V_   V_   _v   V_   _v

I. Write.

1. _____

2. _____

3. _____

4. _____

Around the School

A. Listen and point.

Words
Down
In
Out
Up

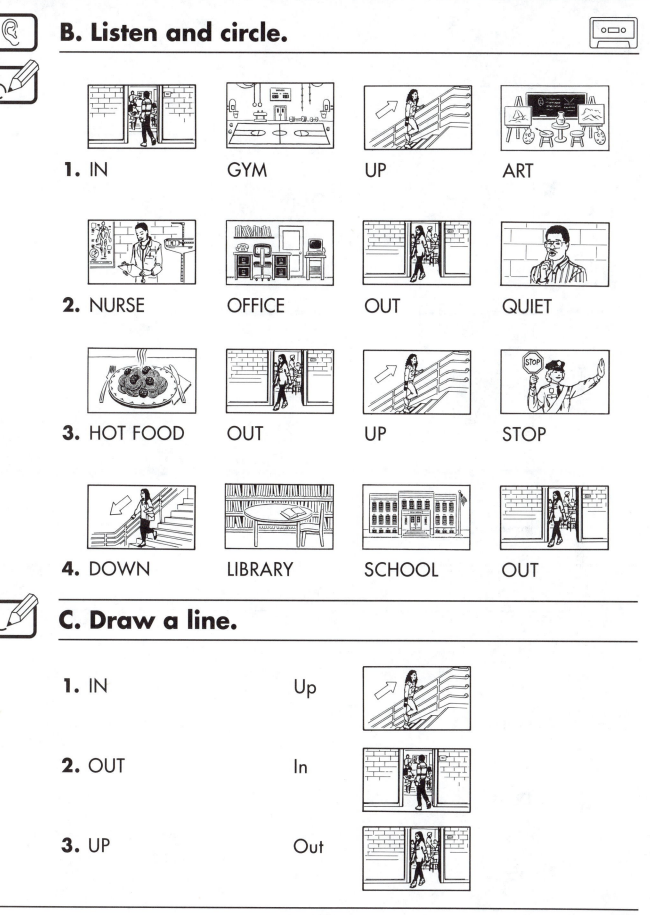

B. Listen and circle.

1. IN   GYM   UP   ART

2. NURSE   OFFICE   OUT   QUIET

3. HOT FOOD   OUT   UP   STOP

4. DOWN   LIBRARY   SCHOOL   OUT

C. Draw a line.

1. IN   Up

2. OUT   In

3. UP   Out

D. Mark.

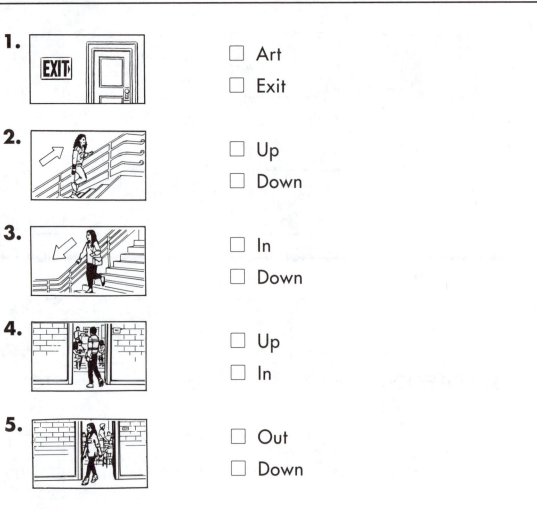

1. ☐ Art
    ☐ Exit

2. ☐ Up
    ☐ Down

3. ☐ In
    ☐ Down

4. ☐ Up
    ☐ In

5. ☐ Out
    ☐ Down

E. Circle.

1. In	Inn	Ink	In
2. Out	Ouch	Out	Outs
3. Down	Don't	Town	Down
4. Up	Upset	Ups	Up

F. Write.

In

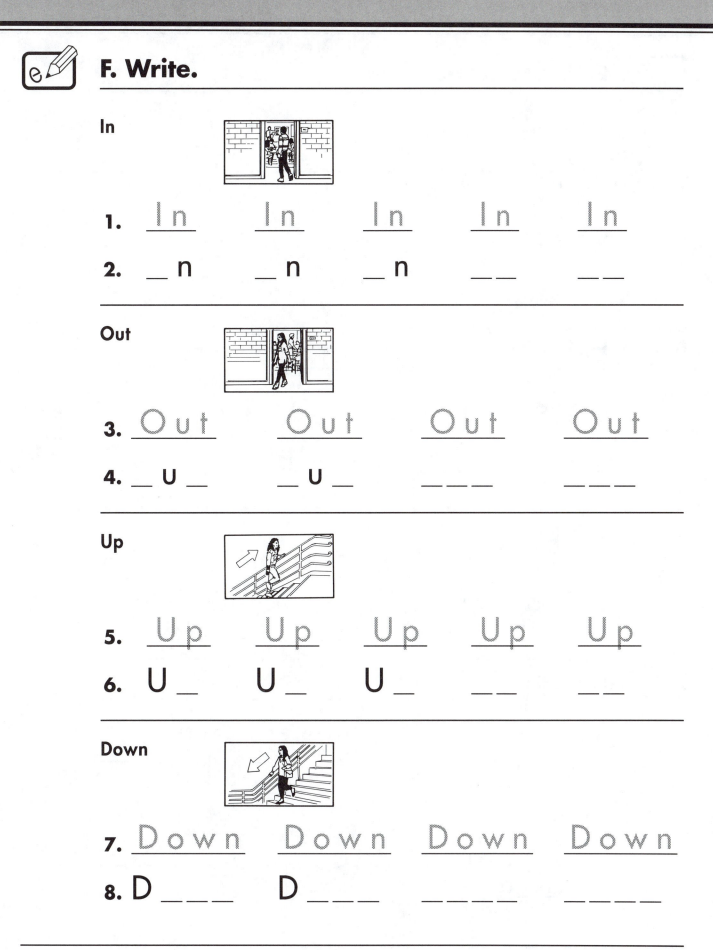

1. ___In___   ___In___   ___In___   ___In___   ___In___

2. __ n   __ n   __ n   ___   ___

Out

3. ___Out___   ___Out___   ___Out___   ___Out___

4. __ U __   __ U __   _____   _____

Up

5. ___Up___   ___Up___   ___Up___   ___Up___   ___Up___

6. U __   U __   U __   ___   ___

Down

7. ___Down___   ___Down___   ___Down___   ___Down___

8. D ____   D ____   _____   _____

57

O   u

D   d

U   i

I   o

H. Write.

1. **U u**   U_   U_   _u   U_   _u   _u

2. **D d**   D_   _d   _d   D_   _d   D_

3. **I i**   _i   _i   I_   _i   I_   I_

4. **O o**   O_   _o   O_   _o   _o   O_

I. Write.

1. _____

2. _____

3. _____

4. _____

J. Listen and point.

31	**36**
32	**37**
33	**38**
34	**39**
35	**40**

K. Listen, point, and write.

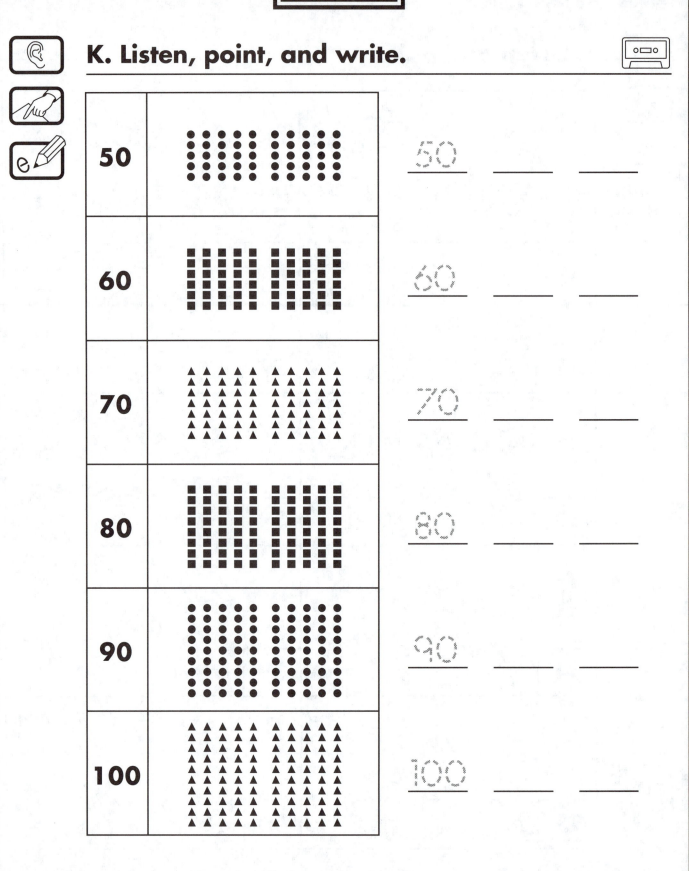

L. Listen, point, and write.

M. Write.

No

1. No   No   No   No

2. __   __   __   __

Yes

1. Yes   Yes   Yes   Yes

2. _e_   _e_   ___   ___

Welcome to Central High School

A. Listen and point.

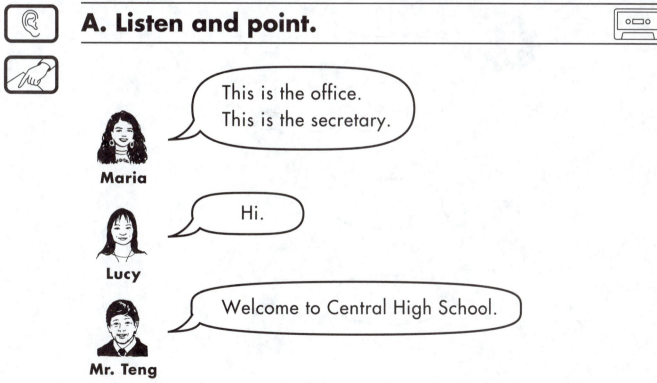

Maria — This is the office.
This is the secretary.

Lucy — Hi.

Mr. Teng — Welcome to Central High School.

B. Read and circle.

1. This is the school bus.
   (high school.)

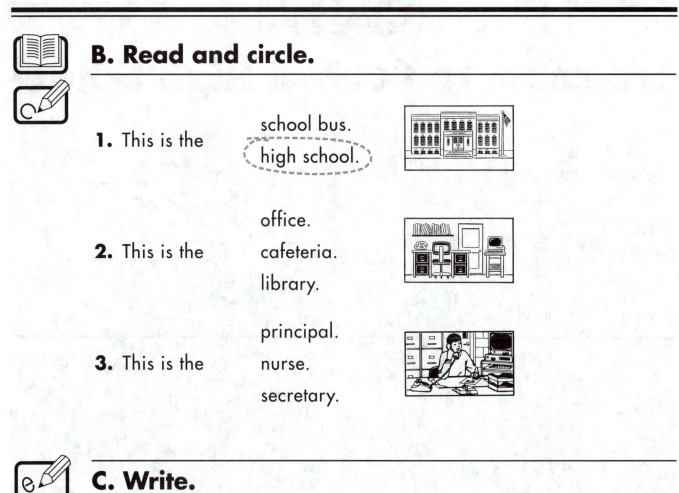

2. This is the office.
   cafeteria.
   library.

3. This is the principal.
   nurse.
   secretary.

C. Write.

1. Hi.

2. H_.

3. _i.

4. ___.

D. Write.

1. This is Central H _ _ h S _ _ _ _ _ l.

2. This is Central _ _ _ _ S _ _ _ _ _ _ .

3. This is the o _ _ _ _ _ e .

4. This is the _ _ _ _ _ _ _ .

5. This is the s _ _ _ _ _ _ _ _ y .

6. This is the _ _ _ _ _ _ _ _ _ .

Words

High School

office

secretary

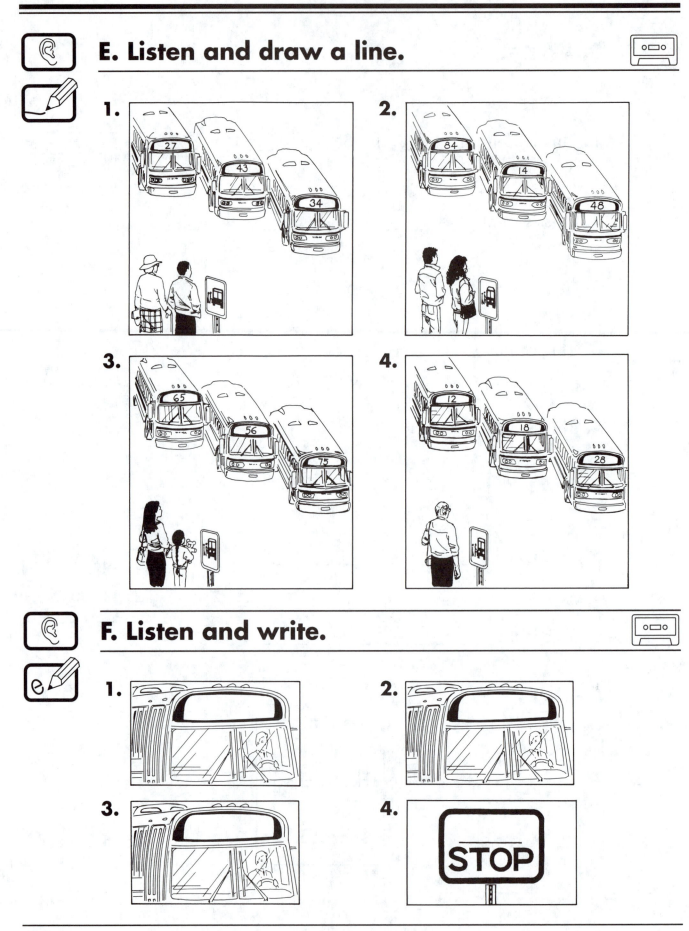

E. Listen and draw a line.

1.

2.

3.

4.

F. Listen and write.

1.

2.

3.

4.

STOP

Give Information

A. Listen and point.

Mr. Teng

What's your name?

Lucy

My name is Lucy Lee.

Mr. Teng

What's your telephone number?

Lucy

351-1452.

B. Draw a line.

telephone number

name

school

C. Listen and point.

Mr. Teng

What's your address?

Lucy

403 Main Street.

Mr. Teng

That's 4-0-3 Main Street.
Welcome to Central High School!

D. Write.

1. name

name

2. telephone

telephone

3. address

address

4. number

number

5. street

street

6. high school

high school

E. Draw a line.

Questions	Answers
What's your telephone number?	My name is Lucy Lee.
What's your address?	403 Main Street.
What's your name?	351-1452

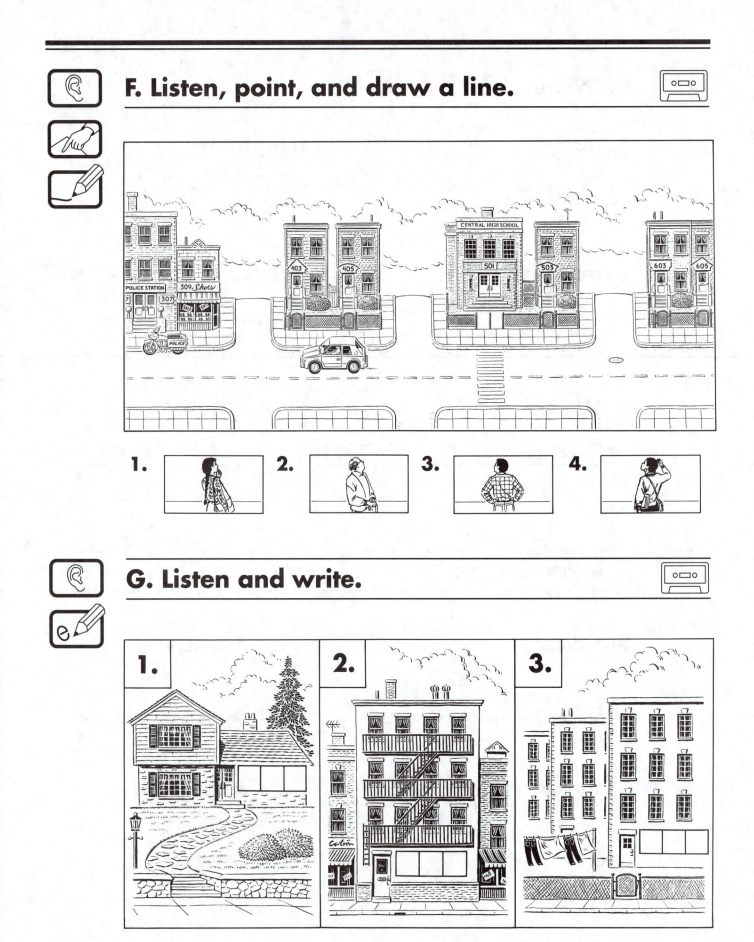

F. Listen, point, and draw a line.

1.   2.   3.   4.

G. Listen and write.

1.   2.   3.

1. Lucy **2. Mr. Teng** **3. Maria**

_ _ _

_____ _____ _____

I. About you. Write.

My school telephone number is __ __ __ – __ __ __ __ .

J. Write.

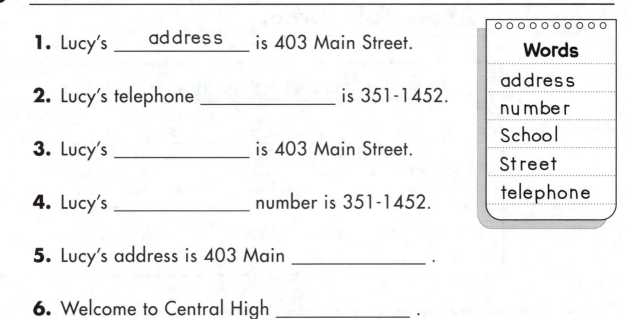

1. Lucy's ___address___ is 403 Main Street.

2. Lucy's telephone _____ is 351-1452.

3. Lucy's _____ is 403 Main Street.

4. Lucy's _____ number is 351-1452.

5. Lucy's address is 403 Main _____ .

6. Welcome to Central High _____ .

Words
address
number
School
Street
telephone

K. About you. Write.

1. My name is _____ .

2. My address is _____ .

3. My telephone number is _____ .

4. My school is _____ .

L. About you. Write.

NEW STUDENT REGISTRATION FORM

NAME _____

ADDRESS _____

_____

TELEPHONE _____

Spell Your Name

  A. Listen and point.

Mr. Teng

What's your name?

Tony Vega

Tony Vega.

Tony	Vega
First name	Last name

Mr. Teng

Excuse me.
What's your last name?

Tony Vega

Vega.

B. About you. Write.

_____

_____   _____
First name   Last name

C. Listen and point.

Mr. Teng   Please spell your first name.

Tony   T-O-N-Y

Tony   Vega
First name   Last name

Mr. Teng   Please spell your last name.

Tony   V-E-G-A

D. Listen and circle.

1. (T) O N Y   5. V E G A
2. T O N Y   6. V E G A
3. T O N Y   7. V E G A
4. T O N Y   8. V E G A

74

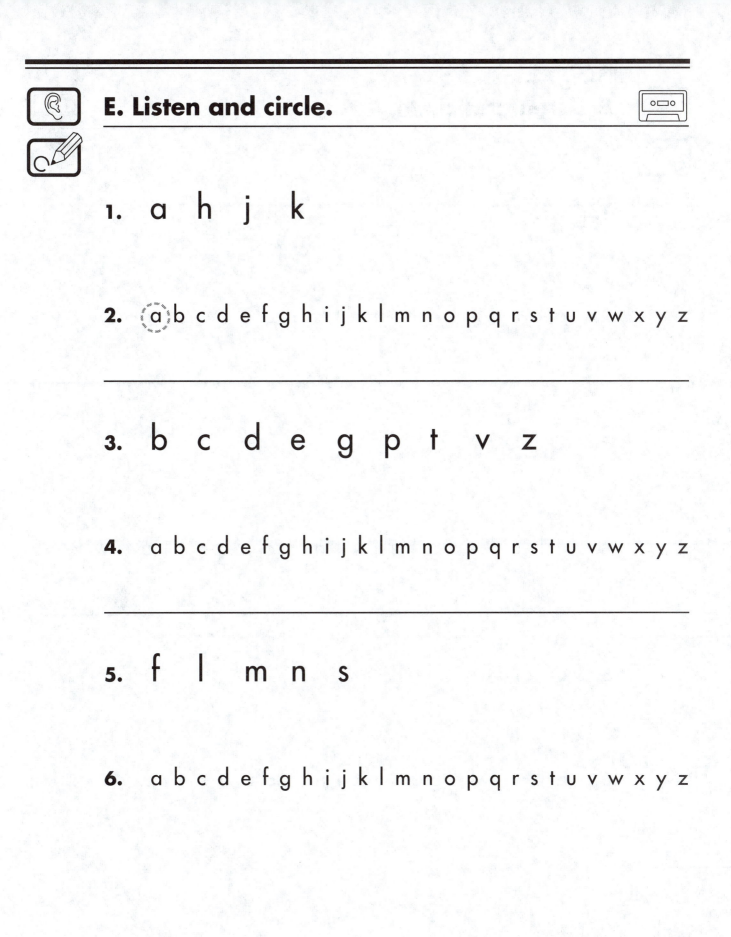

1. a h j k

2. a b c d e f g h i j k l m n o p q r s t u v w x y z

3. b c d e g p t v z

4. a b c d e f g h i j k l m n o p q r s t u v w x y z

5. f l m n s

6. a b c d e f g h i j k l m n o p q r s t u v w x y z

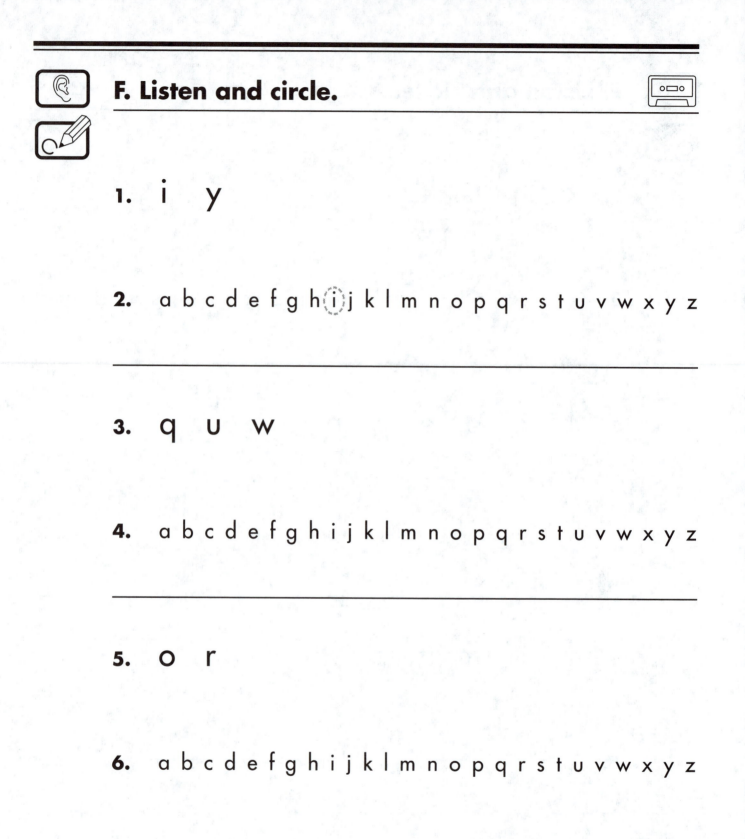

1. i   y

2. a b c d e f g h i j k l m n o p q r s t u v w x y z

3. q u w

4. a b c d e f g h i j k l m n o p q r s t u v w x y z

5. o   r

6. a b c d e f g h i j k l m n o p q r s t u v w x y z

G. Listen and circle.

1. a e i o u

2. a e i o u

3. a e i o u

4. a e i o u

5. a e i o u

H. Listen, write, and draw a line.

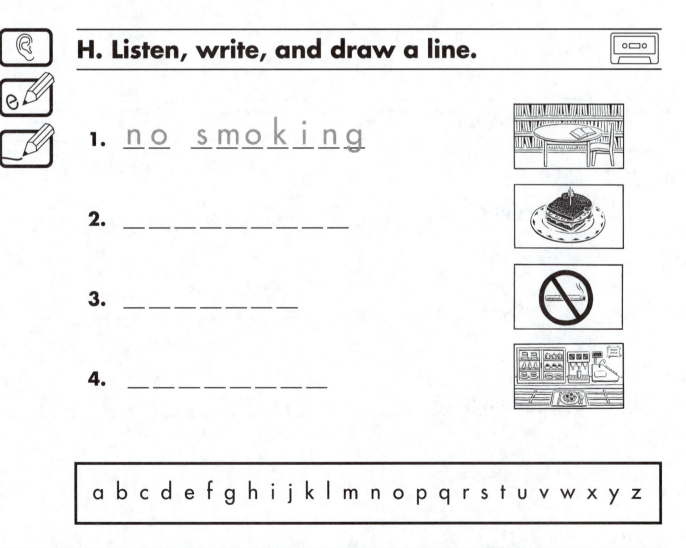

1. no smoking

2. _ _ _ _ _ _ _ _ _ _

3. _ _ _ _ _ _ _ _

4. _ _ _ _ _ _ _ _ _

a b c d e f g h i j k l m n o p q r s t u v w x y z

I. Listen.

1. What's your first name?   Maria.

2. Please spell it.   M - a - r - i - a.

3. What's your last name?   Perez.

4. Please spell it.   P - e - r - e - z.

J. Listen and write.

1. Student 1 _____ _____
                      First Name   Last Name

2. Student 2 _____ _____
                      First Name   Last Name

3. Student 3 _____ _____
                      First Name   Last Name

School Registration

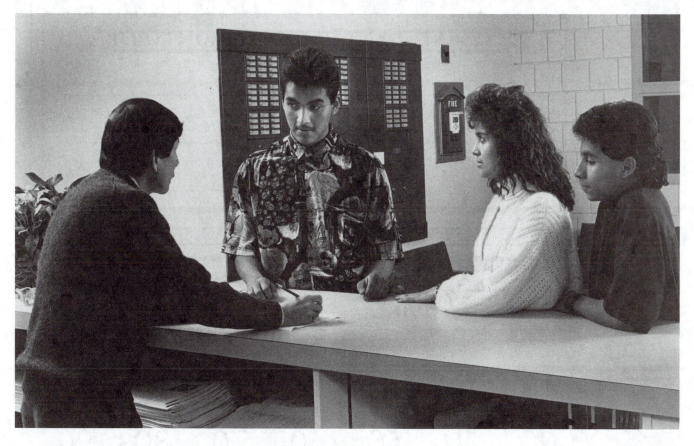

 ## A. Listen and point.

Mr. Teng

How old are you?

Tony

I'm <u>16.</u>

Name	Tony Vega	Sylvia Vega	Mario Vega
Age	16	15	13

B. About you. Write.

NEW STUDENT REGISTRATION FORM

Last Name _____   First Name _____

Address _____

Age _____   Telephone Number _____

C. Listen and point.

13	14	15	16	17	18	19
30	40	50	60	70	80	90

D. Listen and write.

1. _____ age

2. _____ age

3. _____ age

4. _____ age

5. _____ age

6. _____ age

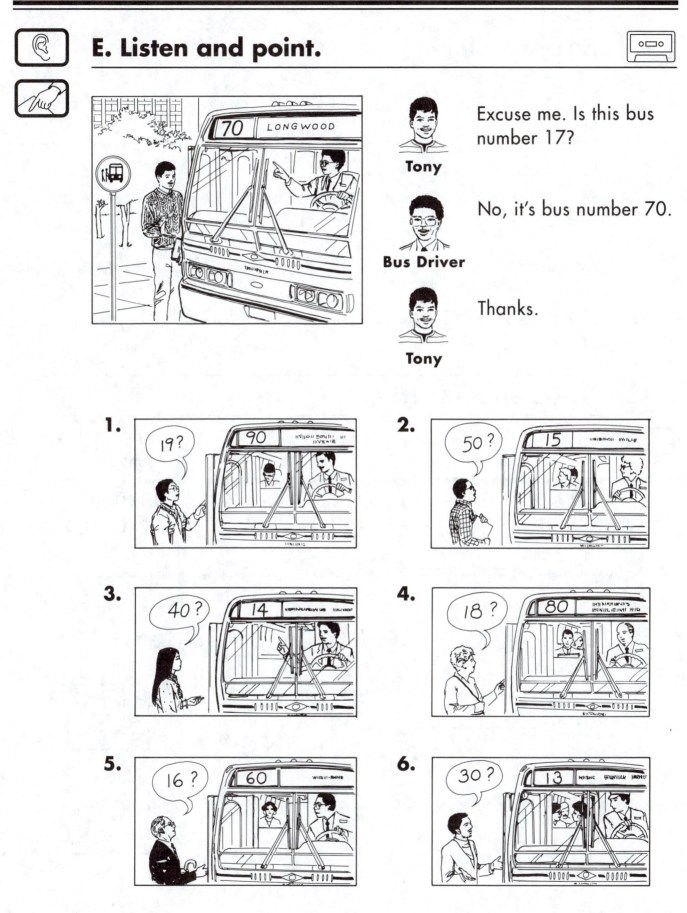

Tony: Excuse me. Is this bus number 17?

Bus Driver: No, it's bus number 70.

Tony: Thanks.

1. 19?   90 LONGWOOD
2. 50?   15
3. 40?   14
4. 18?   80
5. 16?   60
6. 30?   13

F. Draw a line.

First Name	17
Last Name	274-5908
Age	Mary
Address	17 Center Street
Telephone Number	Smith

G. Listen and write.

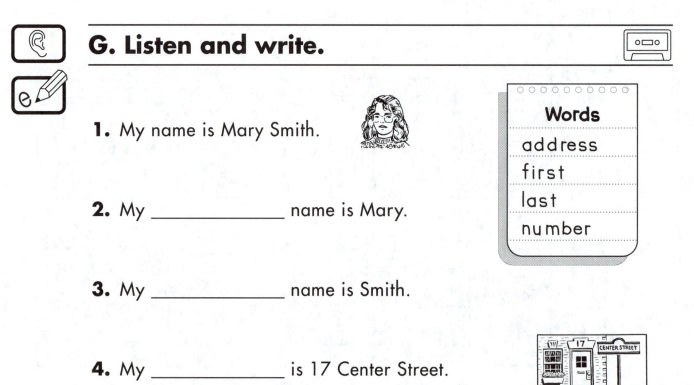

1. My name is Mary Smith.

Words
address
first
last
number

2. My _____ name is Mary.

3. My _____ name is Smith.

4. My _____ is 17 Center Street.

5. My telephone _____ is 274-5908.

Welcome to English Class

  A. Listen and point.

Mrs. Gold

Hello. I'm Mrs. Gold.

Are you a new student?

Lucy

Yes, I am.

Mrs. Gold

Welcome to the class.

You can sit at that table.

Lucy

Thank you.

B. Write.

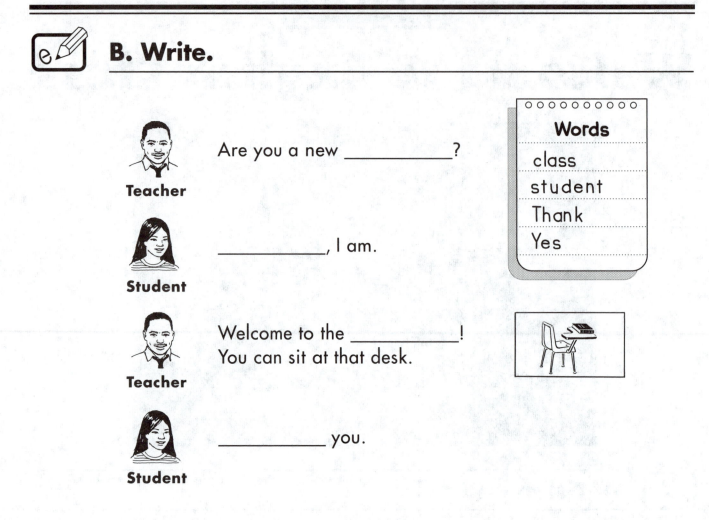

Teacher

Are you a new _____?

Student

_____, I am.

Teacher

Welcome to the _____!
You can sit at that desk.

Student

_____ you.

Words
class
student
Thank
Yes

C. Listen.

The ESL Class

1. Students study English in this class.

2. This class is ESL.

3. ESL is English as a Second Language.

D. Circle and write.

1. _____ study _____ in this class.

  Students   Sandwiches   English   showers

2. The name of the _____ is _____.

            class   gym   music   ESL

3. ESL is _____ as a Second _____.

        art   English   Language   cafeteria

E. Listen and point.

Please come to school on time.

Please bring your book.

Please bring your pencil.

Please bring your notebook.

F. Draw a line.

1. Please come to school on time.

2. Please bring your pencil.

3. Please bring your notebook.

4. Please bring your book.

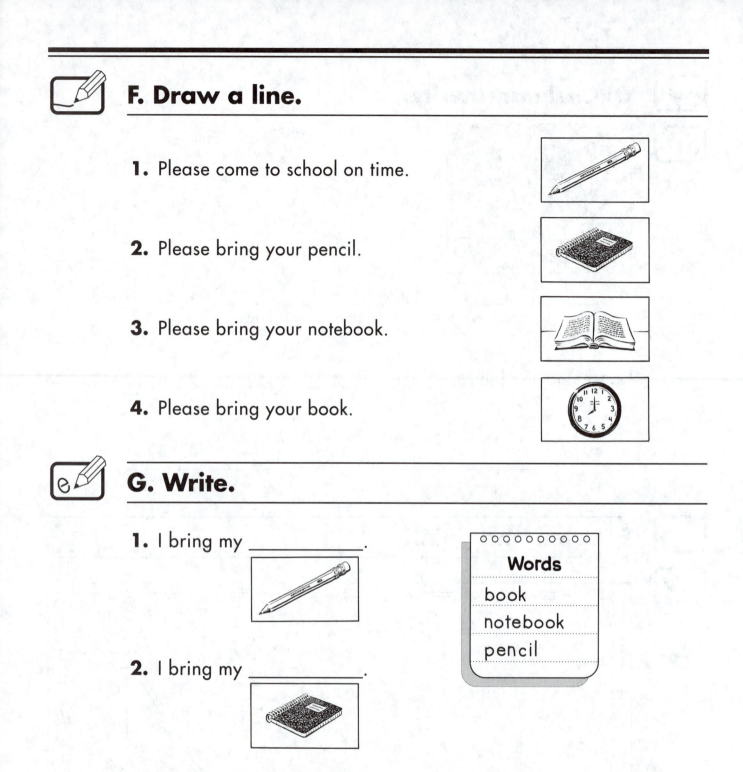

G. Write.

1. I bring my _____.

2. I bring my _____.

3. I bring my _____.

Words

book

notebook

pencil

H. About you. Write.

1. My name is _____.

2. My school is _____.

3. My English teacher is _____.

4. My school principal is _____.

5. My school telephone number is _____.

I. Listen, point, and write.

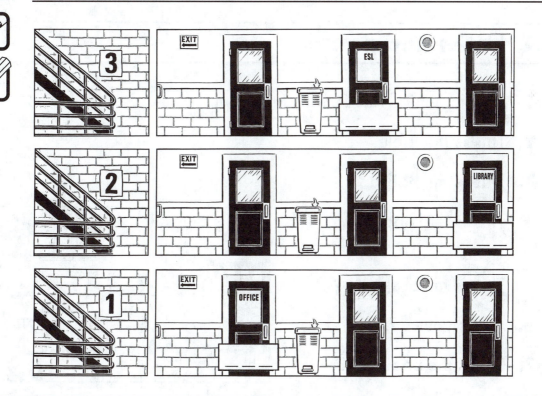

In the Classroom

 A. Listen and point.

1. Hi. I'm Sonia. This is our classroom.

2. This is the table.

3. This is the board.

4. This is the map.

5. This is my desk.

6. That's your desk.

7. That's the bookcase.

B. Write.

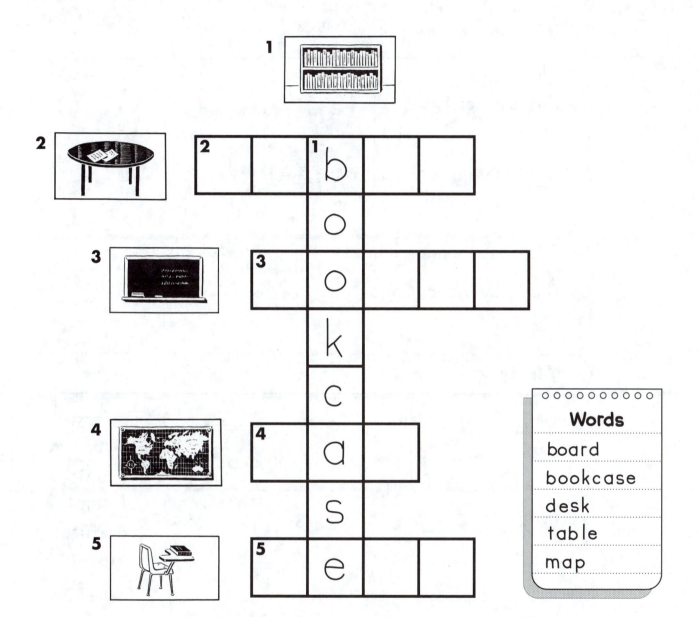

Words
- board
- bookcase
- desk
- table
- map

C. Listen and point.

1. This is my country.

2. This is my picture.

3. This is my story.

4. This is my friend, Minh.

5. This is my friend, Carlos.

D. Write.

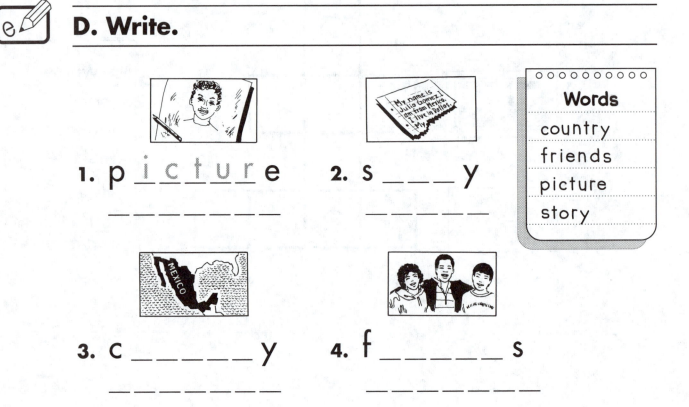

1. p _i c t u r_ e

2. s _ _ _ _ y

3. c _ _ _ _ _ y

4. f _ _ _ _ _ s

Words

country
friends
picture
story

E. About you. Draw and write.

My Friend

1. This is my friend, ___________.

2. This ___ ___ ___________, ___________.

My Country

3. This is ___ ___________, ___________.

4. This ___ ___ ___________, ___________.

High School Classes

A. Listen and point.

1. Mr. Watson is a wood shop teacher.
   He teaches wood working.

2. Miss Smith is a home economics teacher.
   She teaches cooking and sewing.

3. Mr. Jackson is a typing teacher.
   He teaches typing.

4. Mrs. McCarthy is a music teacher.
   She teaches music and singing.

5. Mr. Silva is an art teacher.
   He teaches drawing and painting.

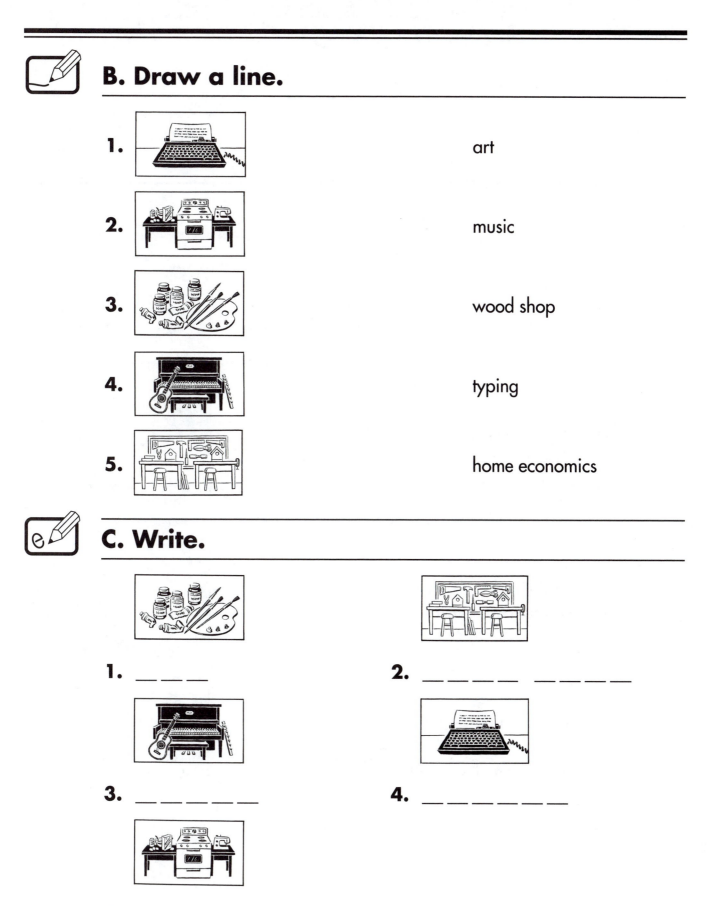

B. Draw a line.

1. art

2. music

3. wood shop

4. typing

5. home economics

C. Write.

1. _ _ _ _

2. _ _ _ _ _ _ _ _ _ _

3. _ _ _ _ _ _

4. _ _ _ _ _ _ _

5. _ _ _ _ _ _ _ _ _ _ _ _ _ _

D. Listen and point.

1. Ms. Kimura is a math teacher.
   She teaches geometry and algebra.

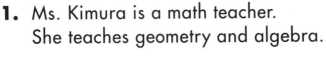

2. Mr. Blue Spruce is a science teacher.
   He teaches biology and physical science.

3. Ms. Fino is a history teacher.
   She teaches American history and
   world history.

4. Mrs. Gold is an English teacher.
   She teaches ESL and English.

5. Mr. Chen is a gym teacher.
   He teaches physical education and sports.
   He teaches P.E. in the gym.

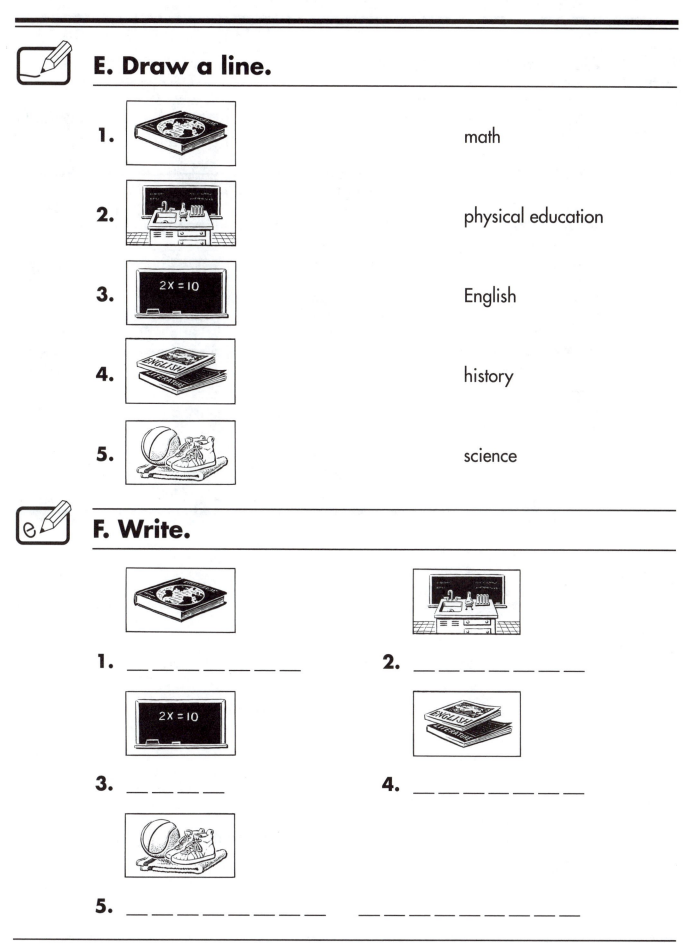

E. Draw a line.

1. math

2. physical education

3. English

4. history

5. science

F. Write.

1. _ _ _ _ _ _ _ _

2. _ _ _ _ _ _ _ _

3. _ _ _ _ _

4. _ _ _ _ _ _ _ _

5. _ _ _ _ _ _ _ _ _   _ _ _ _ _ _ _ _ _

G. Listen and point.

H. Listen and write.

1. Where is room __115__ ?

It's on the __1st__ floor.

2. Where is room _____ ?

It's on the __3rd__ floor.

3. Where is room _____ ?

It's on the __2nd__ floor.

4. Where is room _____ ?

It's on the __1st__ floor.

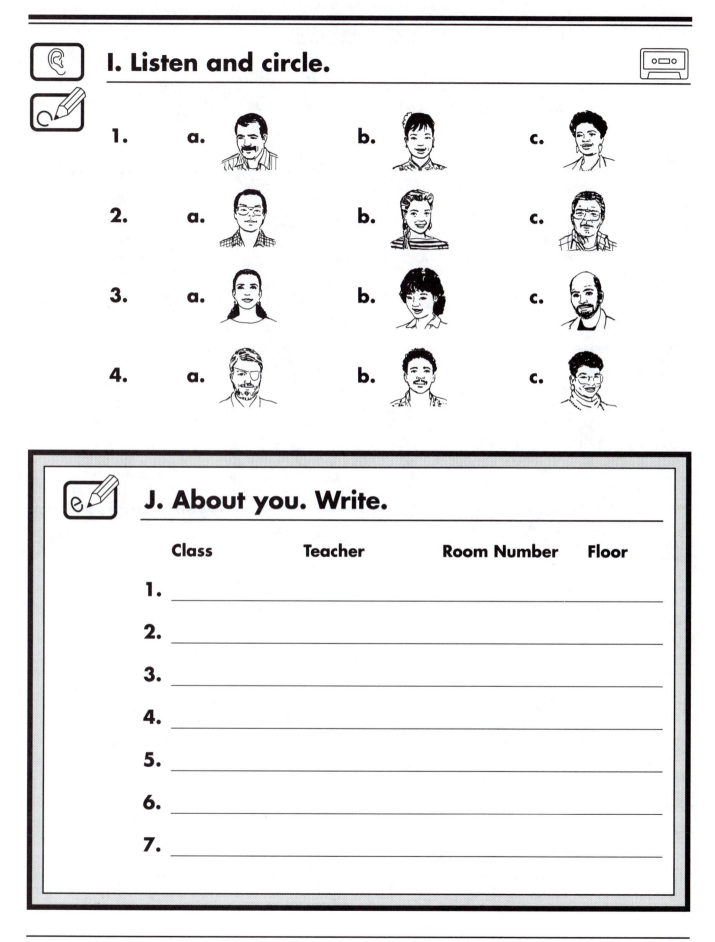

I. Listen and circle.

1. a.   b.   c.

2. a.   b.   c.

3. a.   b.   c.

4. a.   b.   c.

J. About you. Write.

	Class	Teacher	Room Number	Floor
1.				
2.				
3.				
4.				
5.				
6.				
7.				

A School Day

A. Listen and point.

Maria's Morning   Maria is in the kitchen at 6:00 A.M.

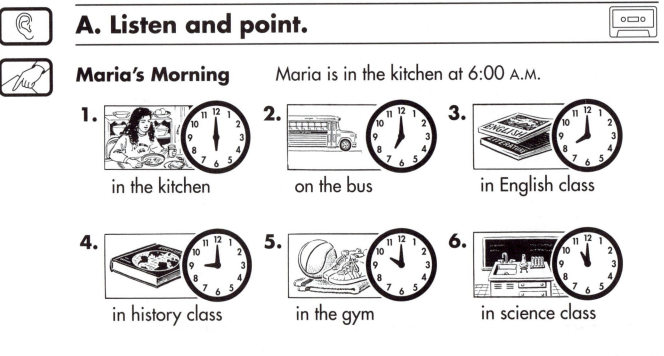

1. in the kitchen

2. on the bus

3. in English class

4. in history class

5. in the gym

6. in science class

B. Listen and point.

Tony's Afternoon   Tony is in the cafeteria at 12:00 P.M.

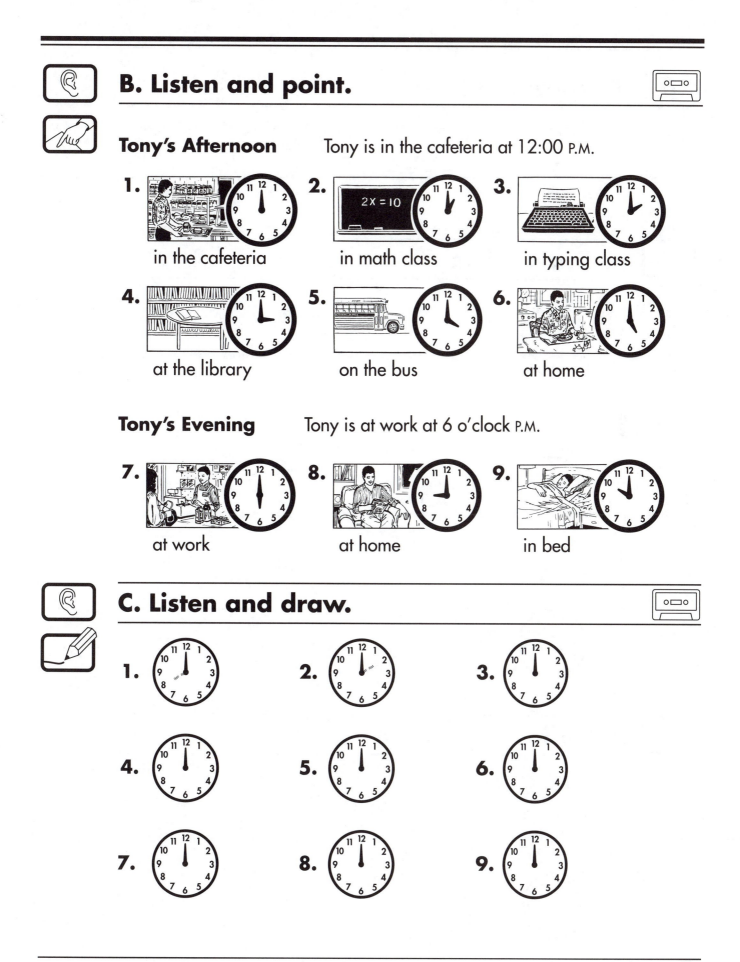

1. in the cafeteria

2. in math class

3. in typing class

4. at the library

5. on the bus

6. at home

Tony's Evening   Tony is at work at 6 o'clock P.M.

7. at work

8. at home

9. in bed

C. Listen and draw.

1.

2.

3.

4.

5.

6.

7.

8.

9.

1. 🕛 = `5:00`   **2.** 🕚 = `11:00`

E. Draw a line.

1. 🕚   9:00
             12:00
             6:00

2. 🕚   7:00
             8:00
             3:00

3. 🕛   1:00
             11:00
             4:00

4. 🕛   5:00
             12:00
             2:00

5. 🕚   1:00
             12:00
             8:00

6. 🕚   10:00
             1:00
             5:00

F. Write.

1. 🕚 _____   **2.** 🕚 _____

3. 🕚 _____   **4.** 🕛 _____

G. Write.

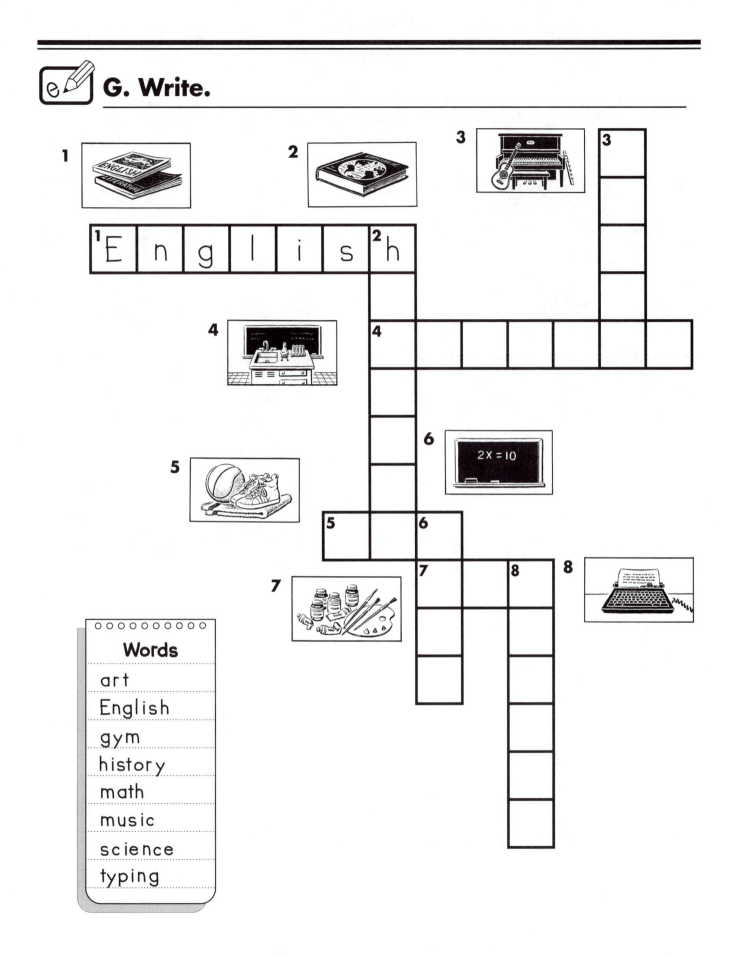

Words

art
English
gym
history
math
music
science
typing

Follow Directions

Class Schedule
Name: Tony Vega
Period 1: Homeroom Room 101
Period 2: Spanish Room 219

 A. Listen and point.

Tony

I don't understand my schedule.

Sonia

Let me see it.

It's 8:00. It's homeroom period.

Go to room 101. It's on the right.

Tony

Thanks.

B. Listen and point.

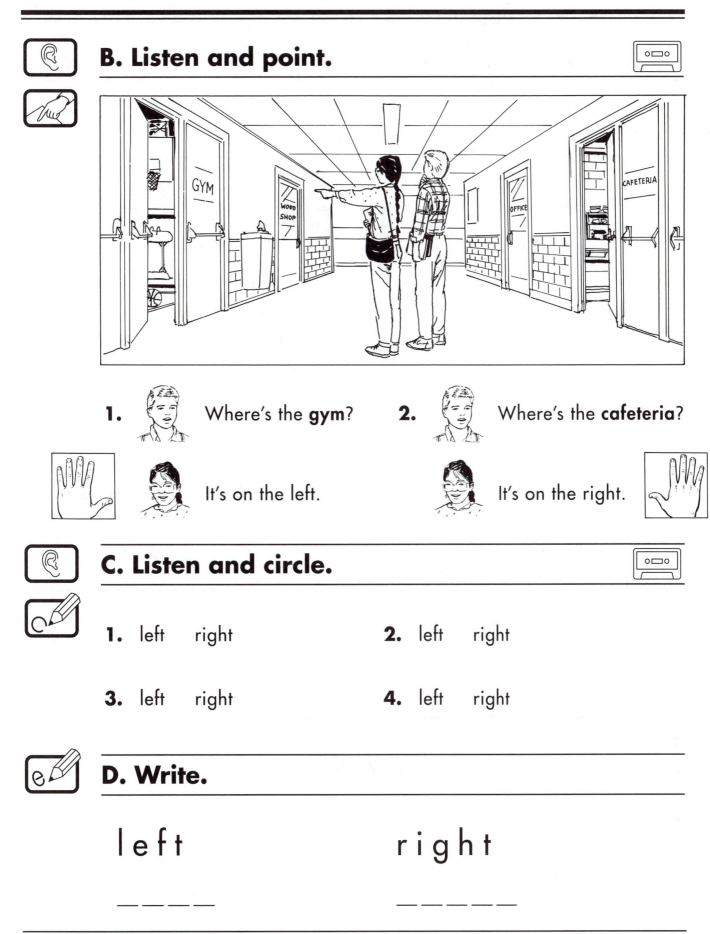

1. Where's the **gym**?

It's on the left.

2. Where's the **cafeteria**?

It's on the right.

C. Listen and circle.

1. left   right   **2.** left   right

3. left   right   **4.** left   right

D. Write.

left   right

_ _ _ _   _ _ _ _ _

E. Listen and point.

1. Where is room **122**?

It's on the left.

2. Where is room **123**?

It's on the right.

F. Look and write.

1. Room 122 is on the _____.

2. Room 123 is on the _____.

G. About you. Write.

1. I write with my _____ hand.

2. I eat with my _____ hand.

H. Listen and point.

 Tom   How do I open my locker?

 Mr. Chen   What's your combination?

Tom   28–17–9

Mr. Chen   Turn right to 28.
Turn left past 0 to number 17.
Then turn right to 9.

Tom   Like this?

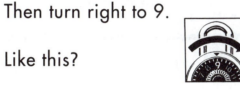

 Mr. Chen   Yes.

I. Write.

Don't tell anyone your locker combination!

Don't tell anyone your _ _ _ _ _ _   _ _ _ _ _ _ _ _ _ _ _.

School Schedules

A. Listen and point.

The Seven Days of the Week

Sunday	Monday	Tuesday	Wednesday	Thursday	Friday	Saturday
Mrs. Gold	Lucy	Sonia	Tony	Vien	Sandra	Milo

B. Listen and point.

Mrs. Gold

We come to school five days a week.

Tony

On **Monday** we come to school.

Vien

On **Tuesday** we come to school.

Sonia

On **Wednesday** we come to school.

Sandra

On **Thursday** we come to school.

Lucy

On **Friday** we come to school.

We don't come to school on the weekend.

Mrs. Gold

Milo

We don't come to school on **Saturday** or **Sunday**.

C. Look at page 106. Circle and write.

1. Lucy has art on _____.
   Monday   Thursday

2. Tony has music on _____.
   Wednesday   Friday

3. Sonia has home economics on _____.
   Tuesday   Saturday

4. Milo plays sports on _____.
   Monday   Saturday

5. Vien has driver's education on _____.
   Tuesday   Thursday

6. Sandra has wood shop on _____.
   Friday   Sunday

7. Mrs. Gold has a big dinner at home on _____.
   Sunday   Tuesday

D. About you. Write.

1. I come to school 5 days a _____.

2. I don't come to school on the _____.

3. Today is _____.

4. Tomorrow is _____.

5. Yesterday was _____.

Words
Monday
Tuesday
Wednesday
Thursday
Friday
Saturday
Sunday
week
weekend

E. Listen.

Teacher: You're late.

Student: I'm sorry.

F. Listen and write.

Teacher: You're _ _ _ _ _.

Student: I'm _ _ _ _ _ _.

G. Listen and point.

1. 8:05

2. 8:10

3. 8:15

4. 8:20

5. 8:25

6. 8:30

7. 8:35

8. 8:40

9. 8:45

10. 8:50

11. 8:55

12. 9:00

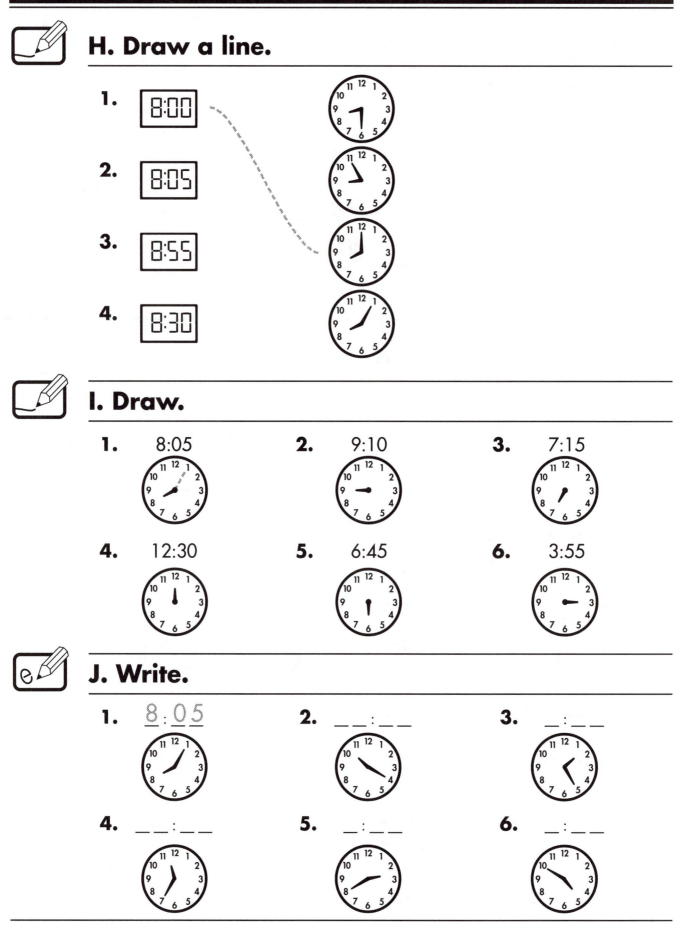

H. Draw a line.

1. 8:00

2. 8:05

3. 8:55

4. 8:30

I. Draw.

1. 8:05

2. 9:10

3. 7:15

4. 12:30

5. 6:45

6. 3:55

J. Write.

1. 8 : 05

2. __ __ : __ __

3. __ : __ __

4. __ __ : __ __

5. __ : __ __

6. __ : __ __

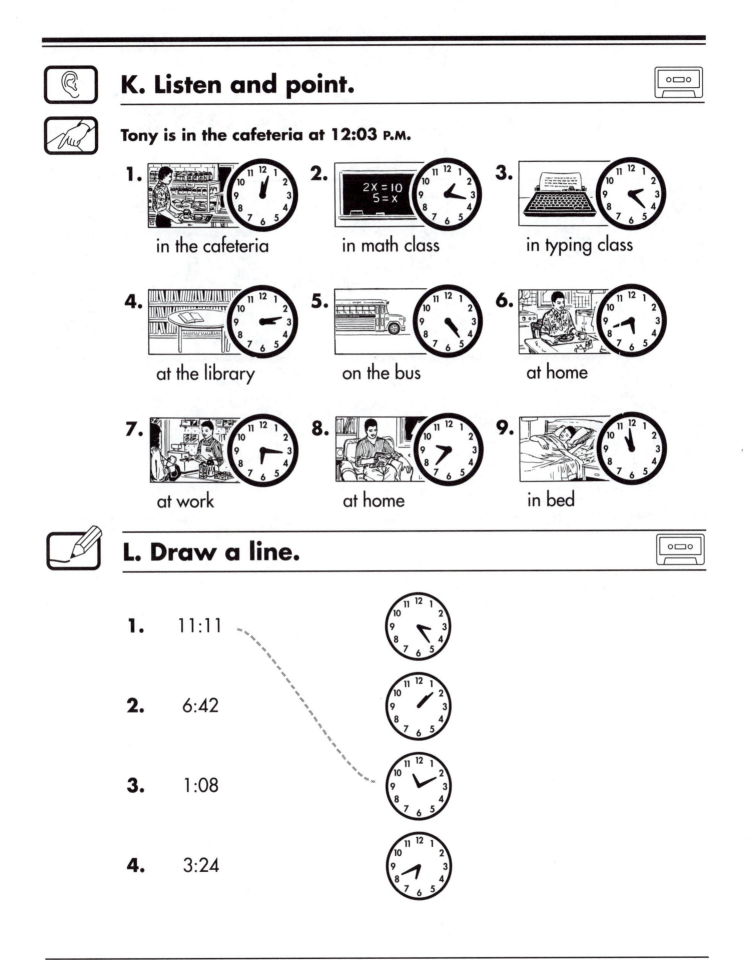

K. Listen and point.

Tony is in the cafeteria at 12:03 P.M.

1. in the cafeteria
2. in math class
3. in typing class
4. at the library
5. on the bus
6. at home
7. at work
8. at home
9. in bed

L. Draw a line.

1. 11:11
2. 6:42
3. 1:08
4. 3:24

Friends at School

 ## A. Listen and point.

1. My name is Mrs. Gold.
I am from New Jersey.
I speak English and a little Spanish.

Hello.

Hola.

2. My name is Sandra Duran.
I am from Puerto Rico.
I speak Spanish and a little English.

Hola.

Hello.

3. My name is Vien Thuy.
I am from Vietnam.
I speak Vietnamese and a little English.

Chào.

Hello.

B. Draw a line.

1.  I am from [VIETNAM]   Puerto Rico.

2. I am from [NEW JERSEY]   Vietnam.

3. I am from [PUERTO RICO]   New Jersey.

C. Draw a line.

1. Chào.   I speak English.

2. Hola.   I speak Vietnamese.

3. Hello.   I speak Spanish.

D. About you. Write.

1. I am from _____.   **2.** I speak _____.

__ __ ____ _____.   __ __ ____ _____.

1.

Pierre

I'm from Haiti.

I like _____.

the sun

the beach

2.

Basha

I'm from Poland.

I like _____.

music

parties

3.

Ramon

I'm from Mexico

I like _____.

books

clothes

F. About you. Write.

I like _____

_____

_____

114

1. Pierre

I'm from Haiti.
I don't like _____.

cold weather

rain

2. Basha

I'm from Poland.
I don't like _____.

cafeteria food

fights

3. Ramon

I'm from Mexico
I don't like _____.

tests

homework

H. About you. Write.

I don't like _____

_____

_____

I. Mark.

1. Pierre likes the
   - ☐ beach.
   - ☐ rain.

2. Ramon likes
   - ☐ homework.
   - ☐ clothes.

3. Basha likes
   - ☐ fights.
   - ☐ parties.

4. Pierre doesn't like
   - ☐ cold weather.
   - ☐ the sun

5. Ramon doesn't like
   - ☐ books.
   - ☐ tests.

6. Basha doesn't like
   - ☐ cafeteria food.
   - ☐ music.

J. About you. Write.

_____

My _____ likes _____.

_____ doesn't like _____.

Write about Yourself

Today is Sandra's birthday. She is 17 years old today. This is her party.

A. Listen.

Lucy: This birthday cake is for you.
Happy birthday!

Sandra: Thank you.
When is your birthday?

Lucy: In September.

B. Write.

Happy   Birthday
H_____   B_____

_____   _____

The 12 Months of the Year

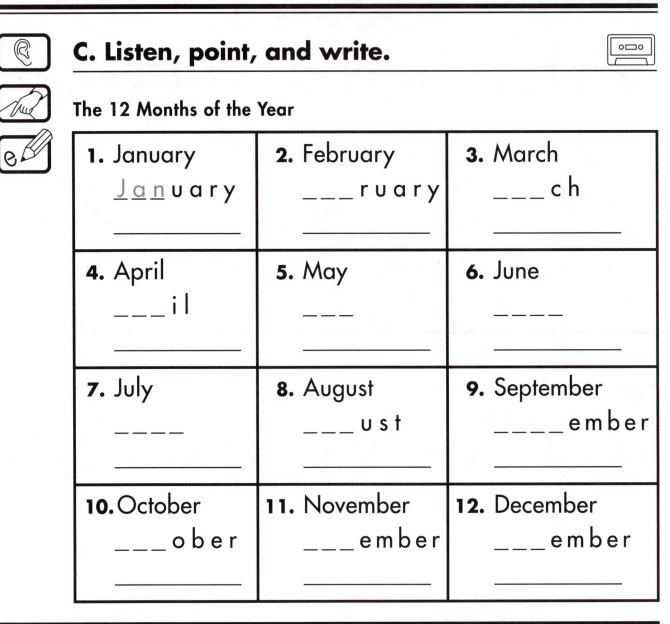

1. January <u>J a n</u> u a r y _____	**2.** February ___ r u a r y _____	**3.** March ___ c h _____
4. April ___ i l _____	**5.** May ___ _____	**6.** June ____ _____
7. July ____ _____	**8.** August ___ u s t _____	**9.** September ____ e m b e r _____
10. October ___ o b e r _____	**11.** November ___ e m b e r _____	**12.** December ___ e m b e r _____

D. About you. Write.

1. This is _____.
month

2. Today is _____ _____.
month   day of month

3. My birthday is in _____.
month

4. My birthday is _____ _____.
month   day of month

E. About you. Write.

1. My first name is _____.

2. My last name is _____.

3. My address is _____.

4. My telephone number is _____.

5. My school is _____.

F. About you. Write.

```
School Schedule

Homeroom Period _____ – _____.

Period 1 _____ – _____.

Period 2 _____ – _____.

Period 3 _____ – _____.

Period 4 _____ – _____.

Period 5 _____ – _____.

Period 6 _____ – _____.

Period 7 _____ – _____.

Period 8 _____ – _____.
```

G. About you. Write.

Class Schedule

Period	Class	Room	Teacher

H. About you. Write.

1. Period _____ I have _____ in Room _____.
number   class   number

2. I have _____ in Room _____.
                        class   number

3. Period _____ I have _____ with _____.
number   class   teacher

4. I have _____ in _____ with _____.
                class   room   teacher

5. Period _____ I have _____ with _____.
number   class   teacher

I. About you. Draw and write.

My Picture

1. My birthday is in _____.
                            month

2. My birthday is _____ _____.
                     month   day of month

3. I am _____ years old.
              age

4. I am from _____.
                  country

5. I speak _____.
                language

6. I like _____.

7. I don't like _____.

Word List

A

address	68
age	80
apple(s)	11
April	118
art	42
August	118

B

bag(s)	23
banana(s)	24
beach	114
bed	99
bicycle(s)	11
birthday	117
board	88
book(s)	23
bookcase	88
boy(s)	13
bus(es)	1
bus driver(s)	70

C

cafeteria	25
cafeteria food	115
cake	117
car(s)	11
chair(s)	59
circle(s)	11
class	83
clothes	114
cold weather	115
combination	105
computer lab	42
country	90

D

day	118
December	118
desk	88
dinner	107
doughnut(s)	47
down	54
driver's education	106

E

English	83
eraser(s)	35
ESL	83
exit	49

F

February	118
fights	115
fire alarm	49
first name	74
floor	96
Friday	106
friend(s)	90

G

girl(s)	13
gym	37

H

hamburger(s)	47
high school	63
history	94
home	99
home economics	42
homework	115
hot dog(s)	47
hot food	30

I

in	54

J

janitor(s)	13
January	118
July	118
June	118

K

ketchup	30
kitchen	98

L

language	85
last name	74
left	103
library	25
locker	105
locker room	37

M

map	88
March	118
math	94
May	118
milk	30

Monday	106
month	118
muffin(s)	47
music	92

N

name	68
no	62
no parking zone	49
no smoking	18
notebook(s)	23
November	118
number	67
nurse	25

O

o'clock	99
October	118
office	6
orange(s)	24
out	54

P

parties	114
pear(s)	47
pen(s)	23
pencil(s)	23
period	102
physical education	94
picture	90
pretzel(s)	47
principal	6

Q

quiet	25

R

rain	115
registration form	72
right	103
room	96
ruler(s)	35

S

sandwich(es)	30
Saturday	106
schedule	102
school	1
science	94
secretary (secretaries)	6

September	118
showers	37
sports	106
square(s)	36
stop	1
story	90
street	68
student(s)	12
sun	114
Sunday	106

T

table	83
teacher(s)	13
tee shirt(s)	35
telephone	6
telephone number	68
tests	115
Thursday	106
towels	18
trash	18
triangle(s)	23
Tuesday	106
typing	92

U

up	54

V

van	49

W

Wednesday	106
week	106
weekend	107
wood shop	42
work	99

Y

yes	62